The Eucharist and the Hunger of the World

Second Edition,
Revised and Expanded

Monika K. Hellwig

Sheed & Ward

Introduction and Chapters 1 and 3-7 originally published as *The Eucharist and the Hunger of the World*, © 1976 by The Missionary Society of St. Paul the Apostle.

Library of Congress Cataloging-in-Publication Data

Hellwig, Monica
The Eucharist and the hunger of the world / Monika K. Hellwig. — 2nd ed., rev. and expanded.
p. cm.
Includes bibliographical references.
ISBN 1-55612-561-5 (alk. paper)
1. Lord's Supper—Catholic Church. 2. Church and social problems--Catholic Church. I. Title.
BX2215.2.H38 1992
234'.163—dc20 92-13317
CIP

Published by: Sheed & Ward
115 E. Armour Blvd. P.O. Box 419492
Kansas City, MO 64141-6492

To order, call: (800) 333-7373

Contents

INTRODUCTION

Does It Mean Anything in Our Lives?

For most Christians the Eucharist is the center of their religious observance. It is a special moment in the week, perhaps in the day, perhaps less often, which has a quality of its own and affects the rest of life. It is not just a time set apart, but it is an action that sets the participants apart in the whole of their lives, however slightly. This much is common experience, though not everyone who participates would describe it this way. To take part in a eucharistic celebration is always an act of allegiance, of self-identification and of commitment, however slight.

With increasing frequency, however, former churchgoers come less often. When young people are of an age to make strong personal decisions, many break loose from childhood training and come no more. At parish lecture series, among religious educators, among groups of deeply committed Christians, the anxiety is voiced again and again that the Eucharist has some kind of pervasive meaning in our lives and we seem to have forgotten what it is. We seem to be living on a heritage from the past that has not quite become our own. The problem is not, of course, that we have forgotten the theology. In fact, in recent times we have been remembering and recovering the rich variety and historical depth of our eucharistic theology that had been lost or obscured. Nor is it a problem of the symbolism. The liturgical revival that has taken place within the past few generations has made possible a simpler, more classic, more accessible ritual, in which it is far easier to follow the language of the symbolism and the language of the words, than it was for long centuries. The dissemination of modern biblical studies and patristic research has also contributed a much richer understanding of stories and themes and hidden allusions, and of all the many dimensions of meaning often contained in individual words.

The problem of which increasing numbers of devout Christians complain seems to go deeper than any of this. It seems more akin to a statement made many times by the contemporary German Catholic theologian, J.B. Metz: the real problem in hermeneutics (that is, in understanding and interpreting) is not that of stating a message from the past in terms meaningful today; the real problem is to find whether the Christian gospel has anything to say in response to the social questions of our day (that is, the questions that arise out of urgent and widespread human suffering today). The sense of uneasiness that we are going through ceremony without substance, does not come from the less generous, the less compassionate, or the less devout, but rather the contrary. It is a far reaching and deeply searching kind of question.

This is the kind of question that is at stake when the contemporary German philosopher, Hans Georg Gadamer, points out that the meaning of a dance is in the first place in the dancing of it, and in the second place in the empathy by which one can enter into someone else's dancing of it, and only in the third place (derived from the other two) in words that can be spoken about that dance. We have not forgotten the time-tested words that explain in rather abstract ways the meaning of the Eucharist. The anxiety so constantly voiced is that perhaps we have never known that meaning in its foundation level of experience, nor even in its second level of empathizing with someone else's experience. Perhaps we have tried to pass on the meaning at that third, derived level where abstract formulations are made, so that we are challenged now to "remember" something that we have never known.

It is this sense of alienation (this sense of being a stranger and not at home in the celebration of the Eucharist) that has prompted some to turn the eucharistic celebration into something more and more like an entertainment in which it is essential to capture and retain the attention of an audience. This is not new to the post-Vatican II era. Liturgical scholars have complained that that has been our problem since the Middle Ages: the Eucharist has been a spectacle, something that people came to view, to view with reverence, with hope, gratitude and contrition, but nevertheless to view, standing outside the action. The purpose of the liturgical reforms has been precisely to change us from viewers into intimate participants. The effect has often been rather to make us keenly aware of the fact that we are coming to view a spectacle, now that the spectacle has been much improved by the retrieval of its symbols.

Therefore, for some people within the church, it is the liturgical renewal itself that has produced a consciousness of alienation, of estrangement from their central Christian action. That may be because their participation was external and superficial before, and the strangeness of the language and ritual concealed the superficiality. But for many it was not so. Many, some of whom were daily participants, could genuinely have said in the words of Vatican II (in the opening passage of the *Constitution on the Liturgy*) that the Eucharist was the peak or summit of their lives to which everything was directed and from which everything flowed. For such people also the liturgical changes have often been distressing and disruptive. Yet, if the liturgical changes were theologically and spiritually well based, the integration of their lives in the Eucharist which so many devout churchgoers already enjoyed should have been confirmed rather than disturbed. If it is not only the clumsy or the theatrical celebrations that have disturbed such deeply devout persons, but (as is often the case) the liturgical renewal itself with some of its central changes, then one must ask whether there is a conflict at the fundamental level of meaning—at that level where we are dealing with the foundation experiences of what it is to be Christian.

There is a story that seems to shed some light on the present predicament. It comes from the hassidic tradition of eastern

European Judaism. In the days of the Baal Shem Tov, the saintly founder of this particular tradition of Hassidism, it would happen that he would take his disciples into a quiet spot in the forest. There they would make a fire, and dancing around that fire the Baal Shem Tov would lead his disciples in the most sublime prayers, lifting them, so to speak, out of themselves in ecstasy. Of course, both fire and dancing have long been symbols of man's relationship with God. We are more accustomed to meeting fire in religious literature, but even for Christians dancing has also been a symbol. From medieval carols to some contemporary religious folk music, Jesus is occasionally pictured as dancing before God, dancing with mankind, even in his death on the cross—an image that suggests total and willing involvement, passionate commitment, a pouring out of oneself.

The story of the Baal Shem Tov and his prayerful dance around the fire in the forest with his disciples, continues as follows. After the death of the saint, the disciples continued to go to that spot in the forest, to light the fire, to dance. But they could not remember how to pray, and their excursions were not the same. Indeed, in the course of time they forgot to dance, and later they no longer lit the fire. Eventually even the place of encounter was forgotten. An era had passed and an experience was now lost.

The story, of course, is not only about the Hassidim. It is about every religious tradition. It is about every kind of discipleship. It is also about our Christian experience of the Eucharist. In his death and resurrection, Jesus has shown us a place of encounter with God, a place that must be reached by a special effort, like the place in the forest. He has kindled a fire for us that mediates the presence of God, and has shown us how to return again and again to rekindle it and enter anew into that moment. He has danced his dance and drawn us into it with him, that we might catch the rhythm and the step and dance it as our own dance. At the heart of that dance is a prayer so sublime, so ecstatic that it can never be captured in words and written down in liturgical formulae or theology books or catechisms. The problem, after many generations and the rise and fall of civilizations, languages and cultures, is to "remember" that inner core of the experience and the action which can not be written down.

If the Hassidim no longer prayed after the death of the Baal Shem Tov, perhaps it was because they were trying to remember what they had never really known at the most fundamental level of personal experience. Perhaps it was because he had prayed and carried them along on his prayer. Perhaps it was because their understanding of the action was of something in which they were "passengers" being carried along, so that the whole prayer experience was really external to them. In the same way, if Christians today are having increasing difficulty with the celebration of the Eucharist, it may be because they have been carried along as passengers for so long. In the course of this, a strange thing seems to have happened. The Eucharist was certainly not always totally external to the participants. It seems that the public or common celebration was external, but that more devout participants infused into it their personal piety, their own inner experience of encounter with God. It was not empty of personal experience, but it may have contained for many a personal experience brought to the Eucharist from elsewhere, not that experience of the dying Jesus into which his earliest followers were drawn both by their historical participation in the event and by his institution of the eucharistic celebration. The more mysterious and remote type of celebration that we had for centuries, allowed quite varied and even disparate spiritualities to be expressed in the same celebration, and even in the same congregation celebrating serenely together. What the liturgical renewal has done, is not to introduce confusion about the meaning of the Eucharist at the fundamental level, but to reveal the confusion that was there before and was hidden.

Now we find that we are trying to "remember" the experience of Jesus himself as he shared it with us. Like the disciples of the Baal Shem Tov, we find that that experience is not directly accessible to us but only as mediated by the followers of Jesus through the ages—mediated by the record of what Jesus was and did in their sight at the beginning, mediated by testimonies of their experience of following him in different times and different situations, mediated by the pattern of community, of worship, of behavior, or organization in which the experience and the convictions have been expressed. The question that we must ask is how one can reach out and touch the experience of Jesus today. The theological answer has always been: we touch the experience of Jesus by his grace reaching out to us in sacrament, in the word of scripture, and in the teaching and guidance of the church. But the question here is one that reaches behind and beyond the theological answers that we are accustomed to hear. It asks how one is to know at the level of personal experience what is meant in sacrament, in scripture and in the teaching and guidance of the church. It asks how sacrament and scripture and church come about in the first place, rather than simply assuming that they are there. The question does not assume that sacrament, scripture and church are products of a past generation whose mode of experience and action does not concern us. Rather it assumes that these three are present human activities in which we, together with past generations express an experience, an understanding and a commitment that are personally ours.

Questions for Discussion

1. What seem to be the tensions or polarities over the meaning and purpose of Eucharist in our parish, on our campus, etc.?

2. How has our own understanding of Eucharist developed since childhood?

3. What questions do we consider particularly urgent?

CHAPTER ONE

Hunger Has Many Meanings

The Eucharist, the action in which Jesus has summed up the whole meaning of his life and death, is so much greater than our experience. We have to try to understand, not as one tries to understand a theorem in geometry by mastering it, totally grasping and comprehending it, knowing it exhaustively. We have to try to understand it as one tries to understand a person, by being present and attentive and respectful and receiving what the person shows of herself or himself, knowing that a person is always transcendent, mysterious, never really possessed or totally known. We have an analogy also in a work of art. A Mozart concerto is never really known exhaustively, or mastered. To be able to play a part in it, to be able to conduct the whole work, analyze its melodic and harmonic structure, be able to account for it acoustically in terms of vibration frequencies and so forth—all this is still not to know it as a work of art. To know it in this latter way is to experience it as satisfying a great hunger of soul, to be swept out of one's petty and selfish preoccupations by the sublime experience of beauty that it offers; to glimpse in it another way of seeing the whole of reality, the whole of life, and to be challenged. It means to anticipate longingly the next lyrical passage and, when it comes, nevertheless to be again delightfully surprised by it.

The great contemporary theologian, Karl Rahner, has expressed this with a good image: some things are understood not by grasping but by allowing oneself to be grasped. This is basically what we mean by mystery. A work of art is always in some sense a mystery. A person is always a mystery. The Eucharist is a mystery. But mystery is very different from magic.

Magic supposes there is no understanding, no entering into the experience, no personal participation or encounter. Mystery invites the fullest possible personal participation and encounter. Therefore, to enter into a mystery one must find a way in terms of personal experience and in terms of bridges of empathy, built from our personal experience over to what is greater than we are. The Eucharist invites us all to the mystery of Jesus, through appropriation of, reflection on, our own experience, as a base for a bridge of empathy that must try to reach into the redemptive death and resurrection of Jesus in terms of the human experience. It is, in other words, an attempt to enter into the experience of someone who reaches far beyond our experience, in such a way as to be able to say "we."

The great question, then, is how we can identify among our own experiences those that provide a base for building those bridges of empathy. The immediate answer to this is that the action and the words of the Eucharist point the way. This is one important reason for the concern in the liturgical revival with the resuscitation of the symbols so that they will really signify, that is, carry meaning that is easily accessible to the participants.

The simple, central action of the Eucharist is the sharing of food—not only eating but sharing. The simple, central human experience for the understanding of this action is hunger. However, the experience of hunger which we all share, should not be simply taken for granted and allowed to slide out of focus in the action. As a child I was given an explanation of the Eucharist somewhat as follows. People need to eat food regularly to sustain the life of their bodies. In the same way, they need food regularly to sustain the life of their souls. In the Eucharist, Jesus provides us with the real food for the soul (which is he himself), therefore we should receive it often and be very grateful for it.

This explanation is certainly not incorrect, but it is too facile a formulation which quickly covers over the depth dimensions of human experience—precisely all those dimensions that must be explored in order to find the way into the fullest possible personal participation. First of all, the explanation described the action as coming to eat, not as coming to share food. It portrayed the participant as a passive and isolated individual, not as an interacting member of a community. Secondly, it did not invite reflection on what is hunger, what kinds of hunger there are, and what food for the soul might possibly mean. This chapter explores the meaning of hunger. The following chapter is concerned with the image we use when we speak of spiritual food or of Jesus as the bread of life.

To be human is to be hungry. Not to be hungry is to be dead. Yet in our contemporary way of life, many peoples of the world including almost all the Christians, have such a high standard of living that they (we) have long forgotten about hunger. In western, technically oriented society we frequently think of ourselves more or less like machines. Mealtimes come and we refuel. Perhaps we calculate the need for protein, for certain vitamins and minerals, and we refuel accordingly. More frequently, eating is simply a matter of habit and of tastes and preferences. Our hunger is satisfied so quickly, so easily, so continuously that we can easily forget that hunger is there at all; it does not intrude itself.

There is one obvious disadvantage to this. One who is never hungry is unlikely to have compassion or concern for those who are constantly hungry and never satisfied. If we are able to think of our own need for food in terms of a machine, then we shall certainly be inclined to think of the needs of starving populations in mechanical terms in which human suffering is not taken into account. Such incapacity for realistic empathy and motivating compassion is a great deprivation of humanity, an inadequacy of personhood, in those who are thus incapable, as well as a crushing burden to those whose suffering is a matter of such indifference to others.

Before we can begin to understand the symbolism of the Eucharist or try to fathom the message it conveys, we need to remember hunger. Perhaps the older discipline in which the

Catholic Church imposed certain fasts on its adult members, should have been adjusted to modern conditions rather than simply be allowed to be set aside without much thought. It is very important to remember hunger, and the fundamental way to know what hunger means is to be hungry. To understand very well what it means is to be very hungry over a long period of time. To understand in starkly revelatory depth what hunger means is to be starving, or to have developed authentic bridges of empathy to the experience of the starving. In a book like this, it is possible to hint, and to suggest. It is not possible to communicate the meaning of hunger, because that meaning is beyond the boundaries of language. That meaning is in a realm where the function of language is no longer to describe and to define, but rather to evoke. It must try to evoke reflection on one's own experience, retrieval of what has been suppressed, appropriation of what has been allowed to drift by without being experienced, remembrance of what has been forgotten. But language can only evoke reflection on what is already hidden or implicit in experience. It is quite possible that there are readers of these lines who have never had enough experience of hunger to be able to make sense of what follows.

Hunger is a total, global experience. It cannot be compartmentalized or tidied out of the way for other considerations. It does not leave the mind clear and detached to get on with its own business while "the body" demands food (as though the body were a separate being). Hunger is elemental and basic. When it is not soon satisfied, it becomes the central business of the mind. It draws the focus of the whole person to the need for food. Well-fed people are often not aware of this. They have had the experience of skipping meals and scarcely noticing it, but this is only because we habitually eat when "it is time" or when we have an appetite, but long before there is authentic hunger. People who have been or are authentically hungry, and never really have that hunger satisfied, know that this is an experience that qualifies the total experience of the person and changes his focus in a brutalizing way—brutalizing, because it constricts, shortens vision, cuts off the freedom to transcend, which is human.

Hunger is a painful experience. It is an experience of need, urgent need. We all know that infants, when hungry, scream and contort their faces and bodies as though being fearfully tortured, and that young children become irritable to the point of frenzy and disintegration of the personal focus they have acquired, if a meal is delayed beyond their physiological tolerance. Adults of highest moral caliber who have volunteered for hunger experiments, have been known to lose their personal focus and morale to the point of stealing food and lying to the experimenters although they could have withdrawn voluntarily and with dignity from the experiment, had their critical facult-ies been clearer. But their critical faculties were not clear precisely because of the hunger itself.

Hunger is, of course, functional. The reason it is a global and urgent, all consuming experience, is that it expresses the most basic need that must be satisfied. It draws the focus of the person to immediate efforts to satisfy the need. Hunger is painful in order that it can demand the necessary response authoritatively. Ordinarily, we escape from hunger by eating. There are other ways, such as hypnosis or ecstasy. There is also a physiological escape, as testified by primitive peoples and by those who have undertaken long voluntary total fasts. When an adequately nourished person abstains from food completely for an extended period of time, hunger soon disappears and the body shifts into a different rhythm until it has used up its reserves. Then hunger returns and there is no more escape from it except by eating or by death. But this experience of the suspension of hunger is reserved for those who are adequately nourished in the first place. For those who are habitually hungry and never really satisfied, there is no safety zone between hunger and starvation; the escape from the torture of hunger is by adequate food or by death. Many never escape torture; they only find enough food to stave off death, and their lives and spirits shrink and shrivel and turn in on themselves in the perpetual struggle to stave off death and to lessen the torture. Horizons shrink to the immediate in time; sustained efforts and energetic steps to better the situation are no longer possible. Horizons also shrink to the immediate in space and social space; it is no longer possible to be concerned with anyone except immediate dependents (ultimately with anyone except oneself), or to consider the problem on a larger community scale where solutions may be sought. Finally, horizons shrink to the most concrete and urgent in sustaining physical life; truth, goodness and beauty are simply swallowed up and subsumed into immediate physical survival.

This is why it may be said that hunger is brutalizing. The human dimensions of life are dormant. When heroes have arisen in a situation of hunger, they have always been persons who earlier in their lives have had their hunger satisfied and have been supported at a level of well-being at which they were free to turn their full attention outward and upward, to become more human, more self-determining, more critically aware of their world and more willingly responsible for it. The hero is never really self-made but begins with the gifts from others that have satisfied his or her own needs. History is full of examples of persons who have been able heroically to transcend their personal needs for the welfare of others, but only at a mature stage, renouncing what they have formerly enjoyed and what has become the foundation of their later human maturity. History records many more lives that have never reached this maturity in spite of all advantages.

Hunger, as has been said, is a global experience, painful, functional, but when frustrated also brutalizing. Beyond all this, hunger is the most basic experience of dependence, of contingency, of the need for others. To be hungry is to experience oneself as insufficient, as having needs, as being unable to guarantee one's own existence. To be hungry is to know in a dark, inchoate kind of way that we do not create ourselves, but are creatures, receiving our existence as gift. Never really to be hungry is to be in danger of forgetting that our very existence is a gift—in danger of forgetting reverence and gratitude to the source of our being, the transcendent creator. It is not by accident that food, side by side with birth and death, has always been a central occasion for human communities to pray.

Hunger brings into focus human dependence on the bounty of nature, and raises the important question about the source of that bounty and our relationship to it. But hunger also brings into focus the human person's dependence on other human beings. Very seldom do we satisfy our hunger directly from the bounty of nature, gathering nuts, fruits, vegetables, grains that have grown wild, or catching fish or game that we kill, prepare and cook over a fire kindled from sticks gathered in the wild woods. We eat bread sliced for us by one person, bought from another, transported by another, baked by yet another with flour ground by still others from grain grown elsewhere in fields cultivated with machinery made by further persons from metal extracted from the earth by others again. Whether we can eat at all depends very heavily not only on crops throughout the world, but also on the relative values that international trade places on food and other commodities, on raw materials and on manufactured goods, on things and on services. We who are habitually well-fed are in danger of forgetting this interdependence and living as though we had produced our own food just because we have earned a cash salary or received dividends on an investment we never earned. Those who are habitually hungry are ever mindful of this interdependence. They may not be critically aware of the patterns it takes, nor able to project the action required to change those patterns; but the hungry know that they cannot be fed without the collaboration of others. They know that their lives are hostages in others' hands—not only their sheer survival but the quality of their lives, the extent of their freedom to be human.

Hunger, then, is a basic dimension of becoming, of coming into being as a human person, of coming to maturity. It is a basic dimension of the creaturely response to being called into being by the transcendent creator. It is a creative force in which the power of God takes shape as the experience of the human person. It is an experience in which one can "feel" oneself being created. It is an experience of being created in interdependence with others. But the meaning of the experience is precarious, because the shape of what each of us actually experiences is largely determined by the awareness and responses of many others—their awareness of their own hungers and the bridges of empathy that they do or do not manage to build to reach a sense of the hungers of others. At that very point in the depth of human experience where our creaturehood is most surely to be discovered and known, many human persons in fact experience only overwhelming, permanent, crushing frustration of their own drive to come into being as persons, because the empathy of those with whom they are interdependent has failed them, and their lives have been excluded from consideration in the interaction.

The reason for this exclusion surely is bound up with the hunger and experiences of satisfaction or frustration of those responsible for the exclusion. When we look at the pattern of distribution of resources in the world, those who are most grasping, who most exclude the hunger of others from consideration, are seldom people or nations who are themselves starving for lack of physical nutrition. Yet they may be people or nations whose own experience has been frustrated by unsatisfied hunger. Hunger has many meanings. The basic physical hunger for food has very close analogies in the needs that people have for other kinds of sustenance, far less easily recognized and identified.

Basic hunger quickly broadens into the need for physical sustenance more generally—the need for warmth, cover, rest, clean air, and so on. But equally pervasive, equally important and far more subtle is the need to be loved into being and the hunger in which that need manifests itself. The experience of that need and that hunger is a general experience, common to all persons, but the interpretation of it depends so much on the patterns in which people have found or failed to find satisfaction, that one might easily have the impression that they are quite different hungers that are being discussed. The following is an attempt to interpret the hunger for love within a Christian experience.

Human becoming is full of conflict. Every child asserts itself absolutely, as though there were no other persons in the world to consider. What the child feels and wants is not what it needs. The child wants, for instance, exclusive, uninterrupted and permanent possession of its mother (who should have no other relationships or obligations and no life or volition of her own), instant satisfaction of all felt needs without effort of any kind, and instant demolition of any persons or things that block the way to such satisfactions. A permissive fulfilling of all the child's wantings, however, would not give the love for which the child really hungers. It would keep that child from any possibility of ever becoming fully a person. To love authentically is to discern the real hunger that generates the superficial wantings. Therefore, to love authentically is to love teleologically, which means to love with the end in view—to love with a vision of what the child can become, to love with a vision of what a person can be. True love is creative, because it calls into being what is not yet. Therefore it not only affirms and supports but also demands and challenges. There is no human becoming without pain, conflict, weary effort, burdensome and boring tasks. There is no human becoming without learning to move out of the limelight, to acknowledge others as persons, to find satisfaction in giving and serving and spending oneself for others. To love any other person truly is to help that person to cross over from the precarious existence of the child's absolute self-assertion to the truly personal and human fulfillment of a wholly generous and engaged, even ecstatic way of being.

The deep, deep need that each of us has to be called forth into the fullness of being by creative love, often makes itself felt in a hunger to be worthwhile, to be valued or appreciated, to have a purpose or goal in life. It has been observed in the contemporary world that those who most insistently complain as adults of finding that hunger unfulfilled, are also those who individually or collectively are amassing and hoarding and wasting so much of the material resources of the world, that others are kept on the verge of starvation in great numbers. It is worth some reflection to try to discern the patterns of this self-maintaining cycle of human suffering, for a person who feels unvalued, unappreciated, goalless, is not capable of generosity and appreciation of others and, therefore, not capable of empathy and concern with their hunger and their need. In the strictest sense, this person needs to be rescued from this dilemma in order to be redeemed or saved, as much as the starving person, whose quality of life is shrivelled and brutalized, needs to be rescued to be redeemed or saved. Both are living a life that is unfree, less than human and marred by needless suffering, but the fearful frustration and torture of the physically starving person can only be resolved by that redemption of the love-starved which consists of a radical conversion from self-centeredness to engagement with and for others.

We are speaking here of being born again, of beginning the process of human becoming more or less from the beginning. We are speaking, therefore, of a creative love that will concretely engage each person where that person stands, physically, socially, intellectually adult perhaps, and wielding enormous and dangerous power perhaps, but psychically or spiritually stunted at an infant level of development—at a level of still asserting oneself absolutely, incapable of feeling empathy or concern for others, demanding total and immediate satisfaction of felt needs, wanting satisfaction without effort, and seeing others as simply instruments for obtaining that satisfaction. No one, of course, can in fact live quite like this, but one can survive by making strategic compromises so as to live as much as possible like this, and people who are born into socially privileged positions can assert themselves very extensively through these compromises. In terms of human development this stance of compromise is qualitatively very different from a progressive surrender of over-assertion of oneself, made in response to creative love and out of a sense of inner stability and worth.

The creative love for which the human person has a deep hunger is a very demanding and exigent force. It asserts the value of the person by what it expects of that person, always somewhat more than the individual at that time sees as possible. Love is creative precisely when it calls for what has not yet happened on the basis of a vision of what is yet to be. A child only walks because the adults expect this before the child can do it. The swimmer comes into the freedom of the deep water only by taking what appears at first to be a terrible risk. To make people feel loved, appreciated and worthwhile, it is certainly necessary to give much, in patience, service, shared goods, genuine respect, praise, affection, and so forth. It is also necessary to demand much and in the demanding itself to express confidence and respect for what the other can become. But to demand is to engage in conflict, and to become involved in the struggle of the other. From a Christian point of view, people in privileged positions in society seem often to be underdeveloped. In a familv in which all the water has to be drawn up from the well, all the food has to be produced by personal labor in the fields, all travel is by foot, and so forth, everyone soon knows and accepts that needs are only satisfied by strenuous physical exertion and by community cooperation, that each person's wants have to be tempered by the needs of others, that the available resources are limited and have to be shared. Inevitably it becomes a way of life and a way of thinking about oneself, a way of understanding personal worth and dignity that is immediately and obviously tied up with the understanding of obligations.

In a wealthy western family today, for whom everything is mechanized and mass produced, there is little realization of the physical effort expended to satisfy needs. The hard, grinding, physical work that is required is being done by South American tin miners, migrant farm workers, certain construction workers, garbage removal people and others whose sweat and toil and burden is hidden from observation, so that it seems that needs are simply satisfied by money and that money comes rather easily. There is little experience of the inevitability of sharing, because more is bought and more always seems to be there to be bought. Restraints are not built into the situation but have to be created by parental decisions. Many parents find it easier for themselves to take children by car wherever they want to go, to let them watch television and movies as much as they want to do, to provide what they ask for, unconditionally and immediately. It is easier because there is no challenge to grow and mature and accept responsibility, and because there is no such challenge, therefore, there is no conflict to deal with and no shared growing pains to endure. On the surface it looks like a highly civilized situation, a real achievement of the human and the humane because things run so smoothly and pleasantly. Yet, we know from the present U.S.A. middle class, city society that many young people who have been raised like this suffer from the sense of goallessness and from anxiety about their personal worth to the point of desperation, that they seldom persevere long even in self-chosen tasks, and that at college age they are still facing those tasks of personal adjustment to limits that were left undone in early childhood.

An authentically creative love gives the person a foundation of personal worth and meaning which is not dependent on possessions (which may be lost), nor dependent on skills and qualifications (which may be more needed at one time than another), nor dependent on status that comes from family and other connections (which indicates that it is not the person as such that is valued). A true foundation of personal worth and meaning can only be dependent on being—on being a human person, willed by God, called into consummating and ecstatic relationship with God, existing and becoming fully human in relationship with other persons and in terms of responsibility to them and for them. A true foundation of personal worth, in a person who is fully mature, needs to be such as to offer the possibility of authentically altruistic action. In other words, it must have grown to a point of being no longer dependent on praise or blame, transcending the need for approval and affirmation. It is this vision of the fully human person that is given to us in Christ crucified, and this is why we are able to find there the key to the redemption of the world from its self-maintaining cycle of hungers and oppressions.

Authentically creative love is in the first instance proper to God, but is in the second place communicated to the human race, which is the image of God in the making. It is a gift to the human race and at the same time a command. We who are Christians see the revelation of both the gift and the command in the person of Jesus and particularly in the event of his death and resurrection, into which the Eucharist continually invites us to enter. It is not by any casual coincidence that the presence and saving power of Jesus is set forth in the Eucharist in the form of food, because it is a response to hunger, to hunger at many levels.

It is because the hunger for authentic love is not only a need to receive but a need to be able to give that we have a human base for hope at all—a foundation for hope in the design of creation. It is because in their true depth the hunger of the starving and the hunger of the (literally) spoilt rich are complementary that we have urgent need to seek redemption from our false securities, selfishness, exaggerated anxiety over self-preservation. We are indeed greatly in need and greatly endangered, but perhaps not in the ways commonly perceived by those who control the fate of nations and economies. Our most urgent need is to unmask the real hunger behind the frantic quest of higher standards of living and more possessions and buying power on the part of those who already have a disproportionately high share of these—the real hunger behind the sense of insecurity that powers the arms race and the huge defense expenditures of the strongest nations. Beyond the unmasking of the real hunger we are in need of a process of conversion from cramped defensive selfishness to an outward focus—a process of conversion not only of individuals but of groups, organizations, institutions, structures from families to nations.

There are intermediate hungers between the hunger for physical sustenance and the hunger for creative love. There is, for instance, sexual hunger, which does not totally fit into either of the two large categories. There is also the hunger for beauty and harmony, which is so important to the unfolding of all persons, and which has a pattern all its own. It is not necessary to discuss all these types of hunger in detail, but in this book two will be presented for consideration because they are critical challenges of our time: the hunger for freedom and dignity, often manifesting itself in the struggle for national independence, which is considered in the following chapter; and the hunger for peace, expressing a desire to live and enjoy God's hospitality in reciprocity with other peoples, which is considered in the final chapter.

Questions for Discussion

1. Does the notion of "many hungers" make sense?
2. Can we identify any that are not mentioned in the text?
3. What seem to be the dominant hungers in our own society, in our own generation, in our children's generation, in our parents' generation?

CHAPTER TWO

Hunger for Freedom and Dignity

The Twentieth century has seen a remarkable development in the communal self-awareness of the subordinated peoples of the world. Occurring spontaneously in many places and situations at once, this groundswell movement is so strong that it is aptly described as hunger on the analogy with physical hunger. Moreover, it is so insistent that it demands a thoughtful response from Christian communities. We do have to ask whether the struggle for recognition, for self-determination, for participation in society with dignity, for freedom from domination by alien groups, and so forth, is integral to the process of redemption which is pictured and projected in the eucharist, or whether these are quite irrelevant concerns.

The question arises in the first place because we live in the post-Enlightenment era. Society in the western industrialized countries is permeated with the assumption that religion is a private matter which should not intrude upon questions of public polity, the economy, the structures of social life, or international relations. At the same time, and interwoven with the affirmation of the privacy of religious faith and life, there is an extensive and equally pervasive invocation of religious beliefs and loyalties to support and sanction existing structures of power and prejudice. In this post-Enlightenment period, therefore, we have reflected on the meaning and applications of our Scriptures and our liturgy in the context of those assumptions. The combination of privatization of the gospel with the invocation of God as guarantor of existing power structures, has led to the implicit equation of civic loyalties with piety and divine obedience.

Against this a veritable chorus of voices from various oppressed and subordinated peoples of the world has raised a protest, expressing not only the hunger for bread, but the conviction that people live by every word that God utters about human dignity, freedom, justice among peoples and peace. Among the materially and strategically privileged this message has been received with much resistance, judged self-serving, grounded in ignorance, unpractical, confusing the religious and the secular content and foundations of hope, naive in analysis of economic and political matters, and for all of these reasons not meriting serious consideration. Yet more and more voices have merged and demanded a hearing.

There is some superficial justification for this response not only in some current academic assumptions about Christian faith and life, but also in the reading of the Gospels and the observation of eucharistic worship. As the Gospels of the New Testament present him, Jesus does not lead a national insurrection of the Jews against the Roman occupation, nor preach about national independence or the overthrow of political structures. There is much in the texts and in what we know of the context to suggest that Jesus was indeed invited by the Zealots, including some of his close followers, to become such an insurrectionary leader, and that he firmly refused. This might be taken to mean that he considered the political context and economic and other injustices as quite irrelevant to his mission of redemption. But such a conclusion ignores some immediately pertinent factors: short of armed rebellion, causing much loss of life and a great deal of suffering on the part of innocent people, the methods available for radical social change were subtle and slow, and mainly by way of community building from the grassroots upwards into the larger structures.

Before concluding from the gospel accounts that Jesus considered the pattern and effect of larger structures of civil society as irrelevant to his mission, we must acknowledge that he was crucified by the Romans after being convicted as a claimant to the Davidic throne, that is as one who endangered the Empire. He was seen by shrewd people who had everything at stake as a dangerous kind of facilitator in a process of consciousness raising and community organizing. The same suspicion surrounded his followers for the first three centuries after his death. Because there was no democratic process of government, no rapid dissemination of information in print or electronic media, no developed means of economic analysis, no statistics or public opinion polls, social change could only be by strategies of violence from positions of power, internal or external to the society, by natural disasters or blessings such as a superabundant harvest which could not be humanly planned, a technical breakthrough which would be unforeseen in itself and in its consequences, or else by slow shaping of consciousness, conviction and commitment, spreading like leaven through small communities into the large society. Both the gospels and the history of the early Christian communities are far more compatible with this interpretation of the concerns and ministry of Jesus than with the interpretation that he ruled out the larger structures of society as irrelevant.

Something very similar may be said about the Eucharist as its meaning is projected and applied to the whole of human life in the world before God. When we observe the eucharistic celebration in most Christian churches today, it looks undeniably "churchy," separate, ethereal, and remote from everyday life. For the most part, we are using special buildings, highly choreographed ritual movements, costume uniquely used for these ceremonies, music that is specific to worship ceremonies, leaders of worship set apart from ordinary people for sacred functions, a script allowing speech only to those with designated sacred functions, and so forth. The very elaboration of Eucharist which solemnizes it and underscores its importance, tends in a subtle way to take away its centrality in the real everyday life of Christian communities. It remains central in what is seen as a religious dimension of life, but this is very different from being central to life itself with all its many dimensions calling for integration of values and priorities towards an over-riding goal and purpose. It is precisely this tendency for the Eucharist to become the center only of the religious dimension which suggests that it does not have relevance for the organization of political, social and economic affairs of the larger society.

Against this we have two very strong arguments, one from the basic shape of the rite itself and the other from the discussion of it in the New Testament. The rite itself, as will be explained at greater length in the subsequent chapters, is in the first place the celebration of the hospitality of God shared by guests who commit themselves to become fellow hosts with God. It is the celebration of the divine hospitality as offered in the human presence of Jesus as word, wisdom and outreach of God. It subsumes in itself the grateful acknowledgement of God's hospitality in creation, but also the recall and renewal of God's liberating intervention on behalf of the *habiru* (Hebrews), the enslaved and deprived who had been kept from peoplehood, freedom and human dignity, and were therefore redemptively called anew to be the People of God, a witness and blessing to all peoples of the earth.

While there has been debate among New Testament scholars concerning the question whether the farewell supper of Jesus could really have been on the proper date to make it that year's Passover celebration, there is no doubt about the legacy that Jesus left to his disciples. He bade them continue to celebrate his fellowship meal mindful of interpreting his death and resurrection and his gift to them in the light of the Passover Seder theme, the theme of the great liberation feast. Exodus which is commemorated in the feast, and indeed made present in its unfinished aspects, is in the first place the national liberation of oppressed people, enslaved, marginated from the economy and society of their time and place in history, treated as less than fully human, denied community identity and self-determination. The word of God by which they were summoned back to life was a word of freedom and dignity in the context of peoplehood.

Even in the acknowledgement of this background to Christian faith and worship, there is commonly a tendency to see this as a one-time event of sacred history, rather than a paradigmatic event, revealing how God judges human affairs, intervening on behalf of the oppressed and excluded to empower them for full participation in the divine hospitality. Yet the New Testament emphasizes precisely this paradigmatic character. In the letters of Paul we find a steady insistence that it is in the restructuring of relations within the community that one can see the grace of Christ operative. Eucharist fails of its purpose if it reflects discrimination between rich and poor such as exists in the larger society (I Cor. 11). Christian faith and practice are incompatible with arrogant claim to special status and privilege (Romans 12), and with maintenance of factions and discrimination (I Cor. 1), and with hypocrisy for the sake of maintaining authority or public image (Gal. 2). All things are to be restored in Christ to their right relationship to the transcendent God (Col. and Eph.) and this restoration is made to look very practical and concrete in Paul's evocation of it.

It is in the context of this theme of peoplehood and its exigences as presented in the Exodus story, the Passover Seder, the gospel narratives (including the Johannine multiplication of loaves and footwashing scene juxtaposed with the Last Supper speech and narratives of institution) as well as the continuing celebration of Eucharist, that we must listen to the cry of the subordinated peoples for life and livelihood, freedom, dignity and justice, and community solidarity and identity. The subordinate peoples include nations under military or economic control of an outsider group, minorities who are not granted effective equal status with the majority, and all racial and ethnic groups who are made to consider themselves marginal to the dominant faction and unworthy of a community identity of their own. The important and urgent question with which every eucharistic celebration confronts us is whether we are entitled to discount the earthly, physical, historical dimensions of human suffering which Jesus recalled in explaining the meaning of his mission and of his death, while we claim to be heirs to a "more spiritual" understanding of our biblical heritage.

It may be argued that every hunger for human necessities is pertinent to the celebration of God's hospitality to us in the Eucharist, but that national liberation or ethnic or racial community identity do not belong in this category. Nation is not a given in the organic order of creation as are family (in some shape or form), clan and tribe (as clusters of biologically related families). Yet this is a reduction of the human to the biologically necessary, as though human creativity were not equally a gift of God in creation. Human creativity shapes not only the world about us but the conditions and quality of our own lives and interaction. The ability to do this is not the prerogative of certain more advantageously placed persons or groups, but of all. To be kept from participation in shaping the future of one's community, to be objects moved by others rather than subjects of their own history and society, to have their labor used and manipulated for the profit of others, or simply to have a negative or derogatory evaluation of their language, culture, race or sex imposed on them, is not only a grave injustice to those who suffer these deprivations, but it is a diminishment of the humanity that is God's gift to them in creation.

Every Eucharist we celebrate demands that we ask ourselves individually and collectively where we stand in relation to God's hospitality in the world—whether we are acting as fellow hosts of God's hospitality in the world or trying to corner a monopoly on it.

Questions for Discussion

1. Does it seem strange to think of Exodus as a national liberation movement of oppressed people?

2. What do we think Jesus had in mind when he led his disciples to interpret his death in the context of the Passover Seder?

3. Does the link between Eucharist and today's liberation movements seem forced?

CHAPTER THREE

Jesus the Bread of Life

Perhaps we are so familiar with the idea that Jesus is the savior or redeemer of the world that we have forgotten to wonder what that means. It is even possible that, in spite of using many words and formulations to explain it, we do not really know what it means at the fundamental level of understanding. Most Christians would readily answer, if asked, that Jesus saves the world from sin, both original sin and personal sins throughout the ages. This is not incorrect, of course, but it does not mean anything at all if the person who speaks the words does not feel oppressed by sin and in urgent need of rescue. Nor does it mean anything if the person speaking the words has not really experienced rescue from its oppression—if the person making the claim that Jesus is savior of the world has really never experienced that Jesus makes any difference to what goes on in the world.

Yet, we seldom seriously ask or answer the fundamental questions. We have discussed how a just God could allow people's lives to be spoilt by original sin, when by definition the persons affected were not responsible or guilty of the sin that caused their troubles. But we have not asked at the most fundamental level of experience what we mean by original sin and what is the difference that it makes. The theological answers can slide by too easily without ever being rooted in our experience. We have said that original sin puts mankind out of tune with God, at cross purposes with God, thereby shattering the integrity of each person (the inner harmony of wants and needs and strivings that make up the person) and shattering also the integrity of mankind. We have spoken of baptism as a remedy for original sin, but the question why it is such seems often to be asked and answered in language that leaves people supposing the whole matter is so far outside the realm of experience that one must simply believe that it is so and not expect to understand anything about it at the fundamental level of experience. In theological language we have given answers, of course, that baptism confers grace and gives people an intimate relationship with God that is like the relationship of child to father—a relationship that is had within the context of the church community.

The difficulty with all our theological language is that it speaks of reality at the outer boundary of what language is able to express. It has been formulated out of experience that is really inexpressible. It makes sense within a community that intimately shares the experience itself and equally shares the effort to bring it to expression. But the process cannot be reversed. We cannot begin with the abstract formulation, and hope that when people hear that explanation the experience will be generated out of the abstract language. We are like the Hassidim long after the death of the Baal Shem Tov; we have to find ways to recapture the experience itself, because the recapturing of the formula is simply not enough.

Christian tradition does offer us resources for this, though perhaps not in the places where we more usually look for theological data or source material. It offers us this in the language that evokes rather than defines or describes—the language of story and picture and poetry. But it also offers us resources in the present living experience of the community in which we share. Perhaps it simply requires more effort to discern what is being said to us in the living experience of the community. A Latin American bishop, unshakeably loyal to the teaching authority of the church and to the Holy See, nevertheless said with quiet conviction that God speaks with one voice that is always infallible—the voice of the poor and the oppressed. The teaching office of the church may stand before the world proclaiming that man does not live by bread alone, but the voice of the poor cries out that man does not live without bread. Not only whether we live, but the total quality of our lives is at stake. The message that man does not live by bread alone, really only acquires a human, experiential meaning when seen as the complement to the message that man does not live without bread.

Our traditions show Jesus presenting himself as the bread of life, for instance, in Chapter 6 of St. John's gospel, where we are invited to try to understand that notion in terms of the manna in the desert, the unleavened bread of the Passover celebration, the wonderful work of the multiplication of loaves and fishes, the hunger that is more than physical and more than temporary, as well as our own experience of participation in the Eucharist of the Christian community. Explicitly or implicitly the appeal is made in that chapter to all these points of reference in human experience, in the effort to evoke recognition and understanding far beyond what can be said explicitly and descriptively about the meaning of Jesus for the hungers of mankind. These points of reference offer some help when we ask, at the level of experience, what it can possibly mean when a person describes himself as food for another.

There is an obvious, though not literal sense in which one person may claim to be the bread of another, when the first is the employer and paymaster, or the gracious benefactor, or the tiller of the soil, or the one who brings home an income, from any of which physical sustenance is drawn. In this case the second person would not be able to eat and sustain life without the mediation of the first. But the connection is extrinsic. In a far deeper sense one person can be a source of life and sustenance for another. Literally and physically this is always true of the mother of the unborn or unweaned child, and it is not accidental that the bible uses the image of the mother to describe God's nurturing of his people—of Israel and of all mankind. Nor is it accidental or unduly fanciful that mystics have spoken of Jesus and his relationship to the church in terms of motherhood.

Beyond the strictly physical sense, one person is the sustenance of another wherever one rescues another from despair and offers something for which to live. What the apostles have handed down in the church in scripture and tradition concerning their experience of Jesus, his death and his resurrection certainly includes this. When we read the New Testament accounts very carefully it is striking that the main testimony they give is that they themselves had come back to life, had been raised from death to a new life, and that they recognized that new life in themselves as the life of Jesus, as received from him in an overflow of his own life. In the experience of having their own lives resuscitated and sustained by him, they receive the revelation that he is risen.

Certainly, their accounts tell us of their own utter, blank despair at his execution, as though their own lives (at least the human and personal quality of their lives) had been snuffed out. But it may be important to look behind this to their earlier experiences of Jesus, to ask what his death meant to them. Jesus was sustenance or food to them even before he died and rose. They testify that the encounter with him seemed to call them to life in a more intense way than they had ever thought possible, and that his presence to them and their dealings with him sustained that more intense life. They came from the lower ranks of a harshly oppressed people. Successive levies of heavy taxes by armies of occupation kept them ground down into poverty. Like any poor and conquered people, living under occupation, they must have witnessed frequent scenes of cruelty and injustice—and kept silence. They must have been collaborators in many ways, by their silence, in the oppression of their own people. They must have felt degraded, humiliated, depersonalized, intrinsically worthless, because they had to learn to survive by being inconspicuous and not protesting, seeing their human dignity and responsibility slowly drained away. They must have been more or less in despair concerning any possible change in the situation in their own lifetime, seeing the inability of the leaders to do anything more constructive than stave off certain further disasters that threatened, and that only by further compromises. They did not record any of this. They took it for granted and assumed we would know what they meant when they proclaimed that onto this scene came Jesus and that even before his death he had become for them the hope of Israel, as the disciples on the way to Emmaus were relating. Anyone who has lived under military occupation knows something of the anguish, the fear, the degradation, the despair. Many minority groups know it in their own country.

When the gospels tell stories about Jesus—about his style, his impact on people, his ways of relating to people, things he said and things he did—they evidently expect that we will immediately experience a sense of relief, release, joy. For those who are as aware of oppression as the evangelists were, this should indeed happen. The gospels sketch for us a man with hope, with vision, with a purpose in life, deeply compassionate and apparently fearless—a man who is not silent before cruelty and injustice, and who does not become an accomplice in the oppression of his people. This is a man, moreover, who is able to evoke and foster the same kind of vision and courage and self-possession in a great variety of persons from all walks of life. What he is gives them a new life and sustains that life. He becomes food for thought—creative, horizon breaking thought—and food for visionary action.

We may ask a further question, not because the answer is written explicitly in the gospels, but because what is written in our experience is always implicit in the gospels as a foundation for understanding what the good news is. That further question is what might possibly constitute one person as the food or sustenance of such an intensified and renewed personal life for others. Anyone reflecting on personal experience will probably realize that there are two ingredients: what this other person is, and how this other person identifies with the one who is drawn and sustained. When one tries to read the gospels without our subsequent ways of thinking about the divinity of Jesus, reading the stories on their own terms, one can see Jesus constantly inviting people to tune in with him because he is convinced they are capable of it. He seems to stress his kinship and affinity with those he calls rather than his difference. He seems to invite them to do something with him, rather than passively be willing to receive what he does for them. In spite of frequent subsequent trends to let the humanity of Jesus disappear entirely before an overwhelming sense of divine presence, it is noteworthy that the saints and mystics of all ages have been held entranced by a sense of common humanity, common human vocation and potential with Jesus, in other words by the awareness of a challenge to identify with him.

Speaking with the Samaritan woman at the well, Jesus speaks of two kinds of water—that which staves off thirst only to have it return later and that which definitively quenches thirst, totally fulfilling the longing. It is a powerful image, because thirst is such an urgent and particularly compelling sort of hunger. The evangelist in this image presents Jesus as the ultimate fulfillment of all human striving. This could be (and has often been) interpreted in a purely individual, spiritualized, contemplative sense. But reflection on what we can discern out of our own experience of being human seems to suggest that this is an incomplete and therefore inaccurate perception of the human person. One does not come to human maturity and fulfillment by receiving alone, but largely by giving. The hunger of human becoming is never satisfied by receiving. Nor does one come to human maturity and fulfillment by some sort of insulated inner event, serenely detached from the social, historical, painful and conflictual demands of the total human situation. Had Jesus himself been able to maintain such serene detachment and uninvolvement in the social and political and conflictual dimensions of human tragedy, he would surely not have been crucified as a political threat.

Jesus compares himself with manna, the food wonderfully given by God to his people in the desert. The story about the manna in Chapter 16 of Exodus is a story about God caring for his people, providing sustenance. It is also a story about doing first the will of God, following his commandments, and finding that when one does that, all needs are met, not lavishly or luxuriously but adequately and simply. This story is further a story about sharing and not avariciously hoarding and grabbing; they gathered and measured it so that all had an equal share, enough, and so that anyone who attempted to hoard or grab more simply found that it spoilt. The story is part of the wistful account of the desert years with their simplicity of life and their lack of class distinctions. It appears to be part of the gift of sustaining food from God, that no one is able to use force or superior bargaining power to enrich himself and impoverish others. The other side of the coin of a good life, renewed and intensified, is that people and nations are not destroying one another by driving hard bargains to impoverish others—that people and nations are not trying to amass goods or military strength in a quest for security and fulfillment which can never be found by this means. When Jesus compares himself with the manna in the desert and calls himself bread for the life of the world, it certainly implies that what he gives is to be received by sharing.

Subtly and unobtrusively, the sixth chapter of St. John's gospel also links the reflections on Jesus as the bread for the life of the world, with the unleavened bread of Passover. The evangelist relates that the feast of Passover was near, and that when Jesus looked up and saw the crowds that had followed him, he turned to the apostle Philip questioning as to where it might be possible to buy bread for such a large crowd, although he himself already knew what he would do. The other three evangelists relate the story, too, and simply emphasize the hunger of the crowds (who seemed to be held as with a magnet and had followed Jesus to a desert place without provisions). In fact the accounts in the gospels of Mark and Luke even seem to suggest some resentment and concern on the part of the disciples of Jesus, that he expected them to share their provisions with so many people, and they would not have enough.

This last point is worthy of some reflection. Christian preaching on this story of the multiplication of the loaves has usually taken it as a straightforward account of a cosmic miracle, that is, a wonderful work of God that seems to contravene the ordinary course of nature and make the apparently impossible happen. Scholarship does not help much in determining whether it should be understood in this way or in a more subtle figurative way. Scholarship can only tell us that it is necessary to know and be aware of the many references and allusions and analogies made, in order to understand the full import of the recitals. It is interesting to see what devout Christian meditation has meanwhile done with the interpretation of the text. While preaching has been inclined to take it as akin to the manna story, in the sense that the extra bread came "from nowhere," some Protestant preaching has seen it as a miracle of grace in the hearts of the participants. This interpretation discerns Jesus coming into a situation where all are asking what they can get and transforming it by his gift of himself into a situation in which all are asking what they can give. It is an exhilarating moment of breakthrough in human experience—a moment of trust, self-forgetfulness, real community, perhaps even of ecstasy. It appears as a moment in which Jesus has triumphantly, creatively, loved them into a renewed life in which they are capable of self-transcendence, in which they glimpse (if only for a moment) the possibilities of a very different human existence from that which they have known—an existence that does not sustain itself at the expense of others. Rather there is here a momentary revelation of existence sustaining others by the gift of oneself, and precisely in that finding ultimate satiation of one's own personal hunger.

Whether or not this is the authentic interpretation, the message of the story of the multiplication of the loaves is clearly that in the person of Jesus there is a breakthrough into a way of life that is constituted by trust and sharing and concern for others, and which echoes the wistful stories of the manna and the classless community of the days of desert wandering. It is, therefore, significant that the fourth gospel links this story to Passover, because, for the evangelist as for us, Passover has acquired new meaning with the death and resurrection of Jesus. In other words, the difference that Jesus makes, the nourishment that his person is for others is linked immediately to his death—to the particular death by political execution that he was to die.

In the Eucharist we use only the Passover elements of bread and wine. But Christian piety from the beginning has called Jesus the "Paschal Lamb," an explosive image that contemporary thought does well to recall. A lamb only becomes food because it is killed. Its "vocation" is to exist for the life of others; in a sense its fulfillment is to be slaughtered and eaten. The lamb for Passover was to be very carefully chosen, certified free of blemish, because its eating was an act dedicating the people to God. The same chapter in the fourth gospel, which makes the link between the multiplication of the loaves and the Passover, gives us a very long speech of Jesus (which the story places in a synagogue at Capernaum) concerning the claim and promise that he himself is the true bread that is given by the Father from heaven. The language of this speech does not shrink from very stark imagery of "eating and chewing" the flesh of Jesus and drinking his blood, and the main point of the recital is the scandal and annoyance of most of his listeners. Today, unless this is seen in the context of the Passover ritual with the lamb, we might totally misinterpret the nature of the scandal or might be confused into interpreting the whole speech and the whole meaning of the Eucharist in a magical sense.

In the context of the Passover theme of the lamb, the evangelist (reflecting already on the existing traditions of celebrating Eucharist which have grown up since the death and resurrection of Jesus) marshals his recollections and his own understanding of what Jesus means, and structures the recital of the story. There is a certain ruthlessness in it. The focus of the message is that it is in his death that Jesus becomes the bread of life for others, and that it is in total engagement with his death that others are to find the ultimate satisfaction of their hunger, so that they will not hunger or thirst again. The whole context implies that there is more than receiving involved in this engagement.

The fourth evangelist gives us another very important clue to the understanding of the theme of the bread of life in the Last Supper account, where he relates the washing of the disciples' feet by Jesus. In the story we hear that he assumed the menial task of a slave, in a society where the slave is not a person with rights of his own but one who exists simply for others. The action would certainly have been startling and disconcerting. The story tells that Peter protested vehemently. Then it relates the explanations that Jesus gives. There can be no sharing in his heritage, in the life that he has to give, unless he assumes the role of the slave who exists not for himself but for others. Further, he is doing this rather dramatic symbolic action to help them to understand the events that are to follow in the next few days. Lastly, he is doing this with the injunction that when they understand what it is he is doing, they must do the same.

This very evocative recital is dramatically enacted in the Catholic liturgy of Holy Thursday. In some Christian communions it is enacted even more frequently with full participation of the whole congregation. It would be tragic, however, if this were seen simply as a pious way of remembering Jesus and the total gift of himself to others. The ritual is certainly supposed to be a symbolic response to his admonition that what he has done is what his followers must do. But the response in symbolic ritual is supposed to evoke an understanding of what the response in the whole of life must be—to live not for oneself but for others. This is the theme of the slave and the theme of the Paschal Lamb.

We may still ask, drawing on our whole human experience as our resource, in what sense all of this makes Jesus the bread of life for his followers and for the world? Certainly, we are dealing with a claim that has to do with the hunger for creative love, but which subsumes all other hungers that constitute human becoming. Jesus becomes the food of life for his followers when they come into a new life and discover that it is by living for others that they find fulfillment of their own being. It is only with this breakthrough that the hunger for creative love is authentically satiated. But the breakthrough is so radical that the third chapter of St. John's gospel, in the conversation with Nicodemus, describes it as being born again, or (more accurately) being born from above. A further explanation is given that only Spirit gives birth to (or begets) Spirit. The new life does not come from nowhere. It is only communicated by one who has it. But one who is born of Spirit becomes Spirit himself and can further communicate that life.

In the language in which this reflection is given, it may sound mystical and remote. But it is actually a shrewd, common sense statement. Indeed, part of the answer given by Jesus to Nicodemus in this story is that so far he has been speaking only of matters commonly accessible to human experience and to understanding by empathy. He has been speaking of a rebirth into a very different kind of life that is possible only if someone who lives that life communicates it. But he is also saying, in this story, that this life is offered to the whole world. His own mission is not to come judging and condemning, but to communicate life, an abundance of it, to the whole world. The matters of which he speaks are matters of human experience because they are concerned with that kind of creative love which we all need in order to come alive, but which is so hard to find.

All accounts agree that Jesus, even before his death, was like a magnet to all kinds of deeply troubled people, but tended to be perceived as a threat by those unaware of deep-seated problems and by those interested in maintaining their privileged positions in the existing state of affairs. But the New Testament also tells us that people who followed Jesus were frequently scandalized when they realized that his concern for them and his sustaining self-gift to them meant that they had to be totally concerned for others and give themselves totally to sustain others. Perhaps they had not realized how intimately his availability in service to others was dependent on his great personal freedom and integration. It was a freedom and integration in which his whole being rested confidently on and in the Father and, therefore, was quite independent of the artificial supports that so many leaders need. He did not need any subtle complicity with those in power, but he did not need either the helpless dependence of others on him. He was looking for people to stand with him and engage themselves in his task with him. He gave life and self-confidence and the sense of being securely loved and appreciated and worthwhile. But he gave them without stint, and that meant he gave them exigently with the expectation that others would fully share with him his way of living for others, thereby in turn bringing others to life.

Jesus is the bread of life for the world in a community sense. The New Testament and the traditions of the church through history do not really show us a vision of innumerable believers all relating individually to Jesus, saved and sustained by him by some hidden inner change and acknowledging him in some hidden inner way. Rather, we see a nucleus community that clusters around Jesus and through whom he often works even before his death. It is this community that is transformed and becomes the bearer of the new life. In the Acts of the Apostles we see that community at first scattered, then rallying in the experience of the resurrection, and then multiplying and penetrating rapidly through the known world. The communities that had received their new life from Jesus did indeed become givers of life in their turn and that very fast.

From the earliest times we receive some very specific testimonies of their experience and their understanding of that new life that had burst forth in their communities as the gift of Jesus and his earlier followers. Those testimonies include accounts of the sharing of goods so that no one was in need and no one amassed more than needed. They include accounts of special concern for those whose bargaining power for goods and services and respect was very small—widows, orphans, strangers, the poor. For them Jesus was the bread of life in the concrete, physical sense that a community alive in Jesus was sensitive and concerned for the needs of others, especially those who could not fend for themselves. There could not be any question of such a community driving hard bargains against powerless groups. When there was a suspicion of discrimination on the basis of language groupings (as told in Chapter 6 of the Acts), or of a distinction between rich and poor which left the poor shamed and hungry at the eucharistic gathering (as told in Chapter 11 of the First Letter to the Corinthians), the apostles saw the whole fabric of the church threatened.

Those who had received the new life in Christ were secure in being loved and accepted and worthwhile. Therefore there could not be any need to feel secure by hoarding at others' expense, or to feel important by having more than others, or to make frantic efforts to fill an unstilled and undiagnosed hunger by all manner of substitute satisfactions such as power over others, special status and privilege or conspicuous consumption. Their security rested in the community. For the most part the earliest communities were poor but not destitute. When there is sharing and concern for the common good there is not usually destitution. The latter happens when people within the society or people of another stronger group or nation relentlessly press natural or historical advantages to drive harder and harder bargains against those whose bargaining power is weak. People who are stronger do this, not because they are strong but because they think of themselves as weak. They feel weak because their innermost personal hunger for human fulfillment is unsatisfied, and they are not willing or able to see this in its true light, but prefer to spend themselves in a frantic quest of what are in the end totally inadequate substitutes. But this kind of community, or lack of it, also multiplies and spreads and intensifies its hold over people.

It is in response to this desperate situation that Jesus presents himself as the bread of life, the true sustenance of true human life in the world. When we speak of original sin, it will be more meaningful if we keep this fact of the social history of the world in mind. The understanding of original sin in later Christian centuries has sometimes been cheapened. The meaning of this teaching is certainly not that because of an isolated act long ago God holds a grudge against all human persons ever since, and punishes them by making their lives hard and complicated by confusion of judgment and disintegration of desires and then making their deaths unbearably bitter. Rather, this teaching tries to express something we all know from our experience; destructive (sinful) deeds are never isolated, but send ripples through families and peoples, through generations and whole civilizations, creating a web of false values, disordered desires, inauthentic relationships and identities, irretrievably tangled injustices. This teaching expresses the realization of most of us, at one time or another, that no person can resist the heritage of sin and destruction singly.

Even Jesus did not claim to do this alone. He called forth life in others so that he could summon ever widening circles of people to collaborate in the radical reconstruction of all human society. As the *Constitution on the Church* of Vatican II has reminded us, these circles are much wider and more elusive than the self-identified Christian churches, and certainly very much wider than the Catholic Church of the Latin West that is in communion with Rome. Jesus, by his life and by his death, has engaged the world in dialog in varying ways and in varying degrees. His self-gift in death received a radical response and answering echo from the Hindu Gandhi as well as from the Christian Martin Luther King, both of whom in a real sense gave their lives and their deaths as food for the life of others, so that mankind will never be quite the same (never quite as desperate) because of what these two men have been. The gesture of the multiplication of the loaves is extended in the world today in WHO, UNICEF, OXFAM, Bread for the World, and such efforts, as well as in church-related organizations concerned with sharing food. In these and many other examples that might be given, the situation is different because a beginning has been made.

The problems created by sin, that is by self-defense and the scarcity of sustenance grown out of control and out of proportion to need, are so vast and complex that an individual person cannot hope to make any significant difference. But every individual today can contribute in various ways to those large structures and activities that are making a significant difference, can put weight as a voter behind those policies and candidates that make a significant difference in the sharing of sustenance in the world, and can add weight to non-consumption and non-participation movements that focus on grave injustices which dehumanize the lives of others. To do so is to become oneself in some measure bread for the life of the world, and this means to live in some measure in tune with the life and Spirit of Jesus. The quality of the Kingdom of Heaven is a quality of life more than a matter of using the right words and ceremonies. Chapter 25 of Matthew's gospel tells us that to fail to respond to Jesus in the anonymous hordes of the hungry, the homeless and sick and imprisoned and oppressed of our own times, is simply to fail to respond to Jesus and to take one's stand outside the realm of salvation, in the outer darkness of confusion and frustration in which there is no hope.

To be nourished by Jesus as the bread of life, means to come to share in his life, and his life is to be for others in the most concrete and exigent way. His life is sustained not only by receiving of the goods of the world, but by doing the word of the Father, which is a creative word uttering abundance of life for all. This is why we may be confident that our churches are built on solid foundations. The foundations are twofold: Christ and the Spirit. Jesus is an event that has radically transformed the possibilities for human life in the world, and the Spirit that bonds us into one community with him is the guarantee that the event has taken root in the human race and continues to grow and permeate the whole. This is the basis of Christian hope, but hope is not wishful thinking. Thc possibilities that we have are totally gift of God, but gift received within our freedom to act and transform and give of ourselves to others.

Questions for Discussion

1. Is it meaningful in our times to speak of Jesus as bread for the life of the world?
2. In what ways have we experienced others as nourishment for our lives?
3. In what ways do we find ourselves called upon to become nourishment for the lives of others?

CHAPTER FOUR

The Eucharist: A Blessing

At the simplest level of experience the Eucharist is a sharing of food, as pointed out in the first chapter. But anyone can easily see that it is a symbolic sharing of a token piece of food, and that this token sharing of food is embraced within a very elaborate ritual. Christians are not generally aware of the levels of history and human expression that have been combined into our present eucharistic action. Yet these layers of history are quite important if we are to understand the full sense of the ritual, and be able genuinely to participate in the symbolic action. These are symbols that must hint and evoke after the manner of poetry because we are at the margin of what language is able to communicate at all. It is not possible to compile a dictionary of the symbols. It is necessary to have a treasury of stories and recollections, to match the historical layers that are superimposed in the eucharistic action.

The token sharing of food is enclosed, first of all, in an action of blessing. But the meaning of blessing cannot be given in a dictionary definition at all without badly distorting the sense that it has and has had for the Jews, for Jesus and for Christians. The bible speaks of blessings in a wide range of situations. In the first account of creation that is given at the beginning of Genesis, God blesses the living creatures, including mankind, bidding them be fruitful, recreating for others the life he has given them, and joyfully taking possession of the realms he has created for them. But God also blesses the seventh day, making it holy and setting it apart from the other days of the week—a day of rest and joy and contemplation of the wonderful works of God that are pure gift to his creatures, a lavish inheritance as the second creation story tells us, given as the common possession of mankind to be held on God's terms.

The bible tells of God blessing mankind again after the story of the flood. The flood is introduced as the outcome of rampant wickedness, whereby people totally disregarded the terms on which life and the goods of the earth had been bestowed upon them. After the flood God blesses Noah and his family in the same terms as in the story of creation, but a covenant is set out much more explicitly than before, designating the boundaries. In the story of Abraham we are told that God promised to bless Abraham, making him into a great people, so that he himself might become a blessing to others—a blessing, indeed, to all the communities of mankind on earth. The pattern of this blessing is repeated after the story of the binding of Isaac in readiness for sacrifice; Abraham is blessed by God, that he himself may become a blessing to others, and that his people may become a blessing to all the nations of the earth.

The pattern of the blessing is important. The story speaks of blessings as really effecting something quite concrete in the world. A blessing is a creative act; it brings something new into existence. It gives an increase of life and of the inheritance that God has bestowed upon his creatures. But a blessing is always expected to make the one who receives it the source of blessing for others; it is not expected to come to rest in its recipient and to end there. Many more stories of blessings by God are told, but these three—the blessings of creation, of the covenant of Noah, and of the covenant of Abraham—really express sufficiently what is meant by a blessing of God. Perhaps few Christians reflect on this meaning when it is pointed out to them that God has especially blessed them with wealth or health or other advantages, or that God has especially blessed their country with a productive climate, a strategic location and so on, or that God has blessed them by calling them into communion with the risen Jesus in the community of the church. Perhaps few Christians reflect that one is not blessed at the expense of others but for the benefit of others.

It is not only God who blesses in the bible. Parents bless their children, patriarchs the members of their household, and people who are senior, or of higher status or in some way themselves especially blessed, bless others in turn. In the story of Isaac blessing his two sons, Esau and Jacob, the content of the blessing is partly like a last will and testament determining how Isaac's power and rights and possessions are to be disposed after his death. But it is also something more than that, because it contains a gift of the blessing that Isaac himself has from God. In any case, the story implies by Esau's wild lament that concrete historical results will issue from the blessing, and it is only much later that Esau finds himself blessed by Jacob's abundance.

A parental blessing is particularly important. Life itself is a gift from parents who are only able to give that gift because they themselves are blessed by God to be fruitful and give life to others. It is not only sheer existence, but the quality of life that is a gift with which parents are able to bless their children in the measure in which they themselves have been blessed. Formal words of blessing, customary in some communities even today, make explicit and more immediately a matter of experience, a relationship that is already there and should perhaps be there in far greater intensity. The relationship of parent to child is one of summoning forth from the other what is not yet there. It is a relationship of visionary hope calling into being and fostering a new creation. But that new creation is not out of nothing; it is out of the substance of one's own life and being. This refers not only to bodily substance, but to time and energy and work, to spirituality and to material goods, to character and reputation, to wisdom and social skills, and much more. The parental blessing is a momentary symbolic action that brings this relationship into sharp focus and puts it within the perspective of religious and cultural traditions and expectations,

The relationship that is so clear in the case of parents is also, however, a more general pattern of relationship among human persons. Much of what has been described is not exclusively the gift of parents but of the whole society in which persons live and grow. Moreover, that growth or becoming is lifelong. In a wide sense we are all called to be parents to one another, to bestow on others the life and blessing with which we have been blessed, that is, to bless others with the substance of our own lives.

In all of the forgoing examples, the blessing expresses a relationship, and it is a reciprocal relationship. This is why we are also told in the bible of human persons blessing God. The expression would be very strange if the action of God blessing the creature and that of the creature blessing God were seen as analogous. They are not analogous but complementary. To bless God is to acknowledge him as the source of blessings, to honor him with praise and thanksgiving for his blessings, to let his blessings become fruitful in one's life and actions by becoming in turn a blessing for others. All prayer is an entering into the reciprocal relationship of blessing with God, making explicit and bringing into focus what must be implicit in the total quality of life. This is why we pray particularly over food, sleep, waking, over birth and death.

In the creation story in Genesis, God blesses not only the living creatures, but also the seventh day, the Sabbath, setting it aside as holy for rest and for contemplation of the wonderful works of God. As Jesus pointed out, however, there is a difference here. The Sabbath is blessed not for its own sake but because it is instrumental in the relationship of the people to God (see, for instance the end of Chapter 2 in St. Mark's gospel). The blessing of the seventh day is the creation of rest and leisure and opportunity for communion with God for human beings, especially those oppressed with working in the employment of others, for the profit of others, and with little opportunity for personal growth in their work.

What is said in the gospels concerning the blessing of the seventh day, which makes it Sabbath for the sake of human persons, is certainly true of all blessings of material things. No increase of life or fulfillment is bestowed upon the things, for they have no life in the first place. Material things are blessed only as instrumental in the relationship of mankind to God and of human persons to one another. A grace over meals, moreover, is not in the first place a blessing of food but a blessing of God who is the source of this food and of all life and sustenance. We may call it blessing in the broad range of meaning indicated above. Within the complementarity expressed by blessing, the grace at meals is the human response of acceptance and gratitude toward the creating and provident God who makes the earth fruitful that all mankind may draw the needed sustenance from it and none grab or hoard more than they need.

The blessing that embraces the sharing of food at the Eucharist is an elaboration of a Jewish table grace. The present form of the Catholic liturgy has restored this, blessing God, the King of the Universe, of whose goodness we have this bread (or wine) to offer, which the earth has brought forth and which human hands have made. (The exact translation varies slightly.) This form of blessing is taken almost word for word from a formulation given in the book of benedictions (*Berakbot*) of the ancient Jewish writings collected in the *Babylonian Talmud*. Though the volume seems to have been put together after the time of Jesus, Jewish scholars think the formulations are a much older customary pattern that would have been observed at the time of Jesus.

The effect of such a blessing is not to make the bread holy but to hallow those around the table who share and eat the bread, making their act of eating a moment of communion with God in heightened awareness and receptivity of his blessings which must not come to rest in those who are here at table but must overflow in them to become a blessing for others.

New Testament scholars (notably Joachim Jeremias) have observed that the gospels regard all the meals of Jesus with his disciples as anticipating the great Messianic Banquet. The image of a great feast or banquet is a favorite symbol of heaven, because a party suggests abundance, joy, fullness of life, overflowing in selfless and unselfconscious sharing with others. It suggests people finding happiness in the happiness of others. When Jesus gave thanks and blessed and broke the bread to share in token of their fellowship with one another and their communion with God, then the blessing of the table grace blended with the parental blessing which expressed his relationship with them, blessing them with the substance of his life and with all that he was and had and did. The bread that he passed to them, when as head of the household he blessed and broke and shared bread at each meal, always in a very real sense contained the gift of himself. And always it was a blessing for them, destined to transform them into a blessing for others. Later they were to express this very concretely in the common meals of the relatively poor Christian communities, the concern that none should go hungry while any had wealth to share, and even in collections sent from one local church to another to relieve the need there.

In Jewish observance at the time of Jesus as now, there is one meal which has a particularly solemn elaboration of the blessing of the table grace. This is the Passover Seder meal. In this the blessings are multiplied and extended to embrace the recollection not only of God as creator and provider in relation to all his creatures, but also of God as the One who has liberated and fashioned his people, shared with them the wisdom of his Law, bestowed on them his election. The meal celebrates and reenacts the passage from fearful slavery and confusion and degradation into the freedom and joy of their relationship to God.

Jesus must certainly have celebrated the Passover meal several times with his disciples in the course of his public ministry. On each occasion it must have been invested for them with the new meaning that his person gave to the celebration, for they experienced him already as a great and reconciling blessing of God to them and to mankind. By his ministry of revealing truth and healing and challenging, he had already opened up for them vistas on a new life and a new manner of community among persons. By being in relation with him they had already come into a new and undreamed of freedom. But the evangelists particularly insert within the Passover context that last supper that Jesus held with his disciples before his execution. In that last supper he is blessing them not only with what he is and with what he has done, he is blessing them with the death that he is yet to die. It is in that death that he becomes the ultimate blessing for others.

Mystics and theologians and others have tried to fathom and to express why it should be so. Classic dogmatic formulations of the church only declare that it is so. Jesus himself is presented in the gospels as saying that, after all, no one can have any greater love than that of laying down one's life for those one loves. But there are many possible ways of doing that in a life of selfless service and attention to others. The question that a Christian cannot escape asking, and the question that the Eucharist keeps placing constantly before us, is why Jesus becomes the ultimate blessing for others in this particular way—by a tortured, public, political execution as a criminal.

Scripture scholars and theologians are coming more and more to the conclusion that the consciousness and self-consciousness of Jesus evolved in the course of his public ministry, and that it was only gradually that he himself began to see the opposition against him hardening and focussing irrevocably on a confrontation that must culminate in his execution by the Romans, unless he either resorted to a violent stand or else backed down from his challenging stance. In this view, Jesus did not at the outset of his ministry expect to die by execution. It was not some sort of eternal plan built into his mission by divine ordinance independently of the historical actions and decisions of the human persons that made up his life situation. Pilate was not a pawn of fate, but a man trapped by other men and unable to shake himself free.

The reason then for this particular form of the self-gift of Jesus for the life of the world is to be sought in the practical decisions and actions of persons in history. But our tradition inclines us to look upon it not as a strange and outlandish accident of history, but as the center of all historical action that is typical and representative of the human situation and of the issues among human persons and between human persons and God. Clearly the challenge that Jesus presented to people was very radical and quite stark. The Sermon on the Mount, the Last Supper discourse and much else recorded in the Gospels of his preaching all testify to this. Christians have seen in the cross of Jesus the central expression of the mercy of God, but also the central revelation of sin. Confronted with the challenge of Jesus, this human society within which he preached and lived, the society which we believe to have been best prepared to receive his message, responded with what may be described as panic. Careful reading of the gospels does not lead to the conclusion that the main actors in the drama of the death of Jesus were particularly wicked people. They gave the same reasons of state, of prudence, of common sense, of the need of self-defense and so on that most of us give most of the time for our actions. This is why the death of Jesus is such a dreadful revelation of sin. What it shows is that our normal procedures, values and policies are so utterly corrupt that they lead to the killing of the Savior, the Son of God, who offers life to the world, who is the ultimate blessing for mankind.

To assume that those responsible for the death of Jesus were outstandingly wicked people is to misread the gospel accounts quite badly. It also leads to a failure to understand the blessing that Jesus gives us in his death and the blessing that is constitutive of the Eucharist. The prayer of Jesus, "Father, forgive them for they know not what they do," is recorded as a revelation of mercy to all of us for the way we run the world and conduct our various societies. But the point of the Eucharist is not to reassure us that we can continue to do things that way, and God will forgive. The forgiveness of God is realized in the repentance and conversion of persons and societies; these are two sides of the same coin. The Eucharist invites us into the ritual reenactment of the death of Jesus in the same pattern as any biblical blessing. We are blessed so that we may become a blessing to others. There is no other way to receive the blessing of Jesus, which is the gift of all that he is and has, than to become ourselves a blessing to others by the gift of all that we are and have to those in need—a gift that must often be made in large social actions by communities and nations.

To understand the death of Jesus it is necessary first of all to look carefully at what his message and challenge was. His message was to look not to self-defense but to the needs of the other; to be most concerned about those in greatest need; not to ask what people deserve but what they need; not to defend one's rights by violence but by a simple challenge to conscience; to be concerned at all times with seeing that the will of God is accomplished in the society, trusting that all other needs will be met; to judge people by what they do and not by the words and banners in which they declare their loyalties; to take no revenge but to de-escalate violence and evil by initiating a different style of life and pattern of relationships; to live simply and avoid grabbing and hoarding and enriching oneself because it does not increase happiness but only makes barriers against others and adds anxiety; not to be worried about saving one's life but always ready to give it; not to seek honors and titles and high positions, and not to be impressed by those titles in others; to listen to religious leaders for their superior knowledge of the scriptures and traditions, but not to surrender one's conscience to them or follow them in infidelities and compromises; to scrutinize all laws and dispositions of the civil authority by the law of God and be ready at all times for civil disobedience; to be prepared to find oneself constantly in a persecuted, despised and ridiculed minority, and to accept this as the necessary stance to accomplish the redemption that Jesus offers.

Any quick survey of the Christians in the world today, their average income compared with the rest of the world, their status within their societies, the policies of the nations and societies that Christians control, their average consumption of meat and scarce resources compared with other peoples, makes an odd contrast with the teaching of Jesus. Such a survey also helps to reconstruct where we stand in the drama of the crucifixion of Jesus because it shows where our entrenched interests lie which we have not abandoned in response to the Christian vocation. Such a survey may be diagnostic of our participation in the Eucharist—of the depth or intimacy in which we are able to receive the blessing of the death of Jesus so as to become a blessing for others.

Most Western Christians, confronted with this kind of reflection, tend to be quite angry and give certain standard responses. They may be worth examining. One common retort is that there is a confusion here between religion on the one hand and politics and economics on the other, the salvation of souls on one hand and the improvement of social conditions on the other; that Jesus did not invite his followers to be poor in fact but poor in spirit, being detached from whatever wealth they may have. This kind of response is as old as the generation of the apostles. The letter of St. James deals with it: there is no meaning in love for a hungry person which leaves that person hungry, love for one who is cold and without shelter that does not supply the necessary clothing, fuel and housing. What was not considered in the Letters either of James or of John (who insists there is no love of God that is not expressed very concretely in coming to meet the needs of one's neighbor), is the possibility we have today to meet the urgent needs of others on a vast social scale undreamt of in earlier generations. Today we are aware of the industrial and mercantile interdependence of nations and of the various chains of causes that lead to abject poverty and starvation for whole populations. Our experience and our understanding of our own human situation in the world today is the foundation for understanding what the good news of the gospel is. We cannot live the public, world-building dimension of our lives devoid of concern for others, and yet claim to receive the blessing of Christ in the Eucharist, because that blessing is precisely to set us free from selfish and anxious preoccupations and make us capable of universal charity. "Bread for others is always a spiritual question," said Nicolai Berdyaev, Russian religious thinker of the early twentieth century.

Another retort is that one does not help the poor by becoming destitute oneself. Of course, the New Testament does not invite anyone to become destitute, but it contains a great deal about simplicity of life, avoiding hoarding and the pursuit of wealth, giving one's unneeded wealth to the poor, sharing at all times with those in need, and using great diligence to curb the greed and the lust for power that are so insidiously pervasive in all human society. Beyond this, however, the Letter to the Hebrews suggests and Christian piety has articulated clearly, that to understand in depth what is really wrong with the world one does have to "empty oneself" of privilege, and experience what is experienced by the oppressed. From a position of privilege, the world as it now is does not seem so bad as to need any drastic measures toward change; it is only from the position of those at the bottom of the society, kicked and crushed and trampled, that the sinful patterns of society are experienced as intolerable and in desperately urgent need of change. The self-gift of Jesus comes to us as one in which he blesses us with his death on the cross. It is the sign, as German Catholic theologian J. B. Metz has said, that it is possible to rewrite history upside-down from the point of view of the vanquished. Jesus himself has plumbed the very depths of oppression in order to "remember," to bring to vivid awareness the "unfinished agenda" of history, the experience of what is wrong. The blessing with which he blesses us in the Eucharist is the invitation and the empowerment to enter into the experience with him in his death, and only from that experience of ultimate suffering and despair to enter into the hope that the Resurrection holds for the future history of the world.

What the Letter to the Hebrews says of Jesus, Christian piety has echoed from early times by interpreting the Beatitudes of the Sermon on the Mount in a way in which they seem not originally to have been intended—as an invitation to share personally and by voluntary renunciation the lot of the marginated and the oppressed. The original sense of the Beatitudes seems to have been encouragement to the poor and the oppressed and suffering because relief of their suffering was at hand. From very early times saints and heroes of the Christian tradition understood it as an invitation to take upon themselves the sufferings of the oppressed, and often this very step led to a large scale social change to eliminate certain forms of suffering—the slavery of prisoners of war, the abandonment of lepers, of the sick poor, of orphans and so on.

A further retort is that there will never be an end to poverty and wars because that is how the world runs and Jesus himself acknowledged it when he said before his death, "The poor you have always with you." Seen in its context, the quotation of the words of Jesus from the twelfth chapter of St. John's gospel has a very different connotation. It is a rebuke to Judas for his avarice and misappropriation of funds that indeed should have been disbursed to the poor, but at the same time is a rebuke to him for the hypocrisy of his complaint against Mary who poured precious perfume over the feet of Jesus. The intent of the sentence from which the quotation is taken is so clear within the context that it is very strange that this clause is so often quoted in isolation from its context to exonerate Christians of responsibility for manmade crises of poverty in the world. The whole burden of the Christian gospel is that the world is in a state of sin and selfishness not willed by God and that Jesus has made possible and has himself begun the task of converting the world with all its structures and relationships and values to the will of God—a task he intends to complete in and through our free and creative participation. There were two long periods of time in the history of the world when men of common sense, including some earnest Christians, solemnly maintained that the economy of society could no wise function without slavery. History has shown that a creative modification of working and bargaining patterns renders slavery unnecessary and even unprofitable.

More subtly, the objection to a far-reaching social understanding of the gospel has taken the form: there will never be an end to poverty because no amount of good will can make people equal in industry, skill, intelligence, good health and longevity and so on. The gospel does not say anywhere that there must be no inequality, only that there must be no one in need and (in the Acts of the Apostles) that a Christian society is structured so that the needs of all are amply taken care of without embarrassment or need for begging. After centuries of Christianity, with the message of sharing and simplicity of life, preached and enacted in the Eucharist, one would expect that in Christian nations the difference between rich and poor would no longer be so great and that the poor would at least not be destitute. The abject misery of barrios, haciendas and favelas of Latin America and the long discouraging fight of the migrant farmworkers, the rural poor, and the black ghetto dwellers of the United States of America, give the lie to that expectation.

In fact those who become very wealthy in our wealthy nations, do so not by industry and skill but by investment of capital. That means that they become wealthy by the work of others not by the salary they draw for their own work, with very few exceptions where the salary is artificially inflated and in fact is generated by the work of others. We have become so accustomed to this that we have quite forgotten to scrutinize it by Christian values and goals. To enrich oneself by the work of others is a modified form of slave ownership. It is possible only in a society that has no qualms about pressing hard bargains against people unfortunate enough to be forced to accept harsh and unfavorable terms. Today scripture scholars are reminding us that even long before Jesus, the Law and the Prophets of Israel were sharply critical of such practices and placed severe curbs on them. Land, the only form of capital then acknowledged, could not be transferred in perpetuity; only its use for a span of years could be transferred, after which the land reverted to the family to whom it had originally been assigned, for the land belonged to the Lord who decreed that it be shared fairly among all his people. Loans could not accumulate interest indefinitely but were totally remitted after a span of years. A family that had to sell itself into servitude to satisfy debts must be liberated after a limited span of years.

The Church continued this stance for many centuries in its prohibition of usury, that is, interest on loans. It changed its stance when a distinction could be made between personal (consumer) loans and capital (investment) loans, in particular with the rise of banking. Today money and the functions of money in society again have developed so far that the moral issues have arisen with a new and desperate urgency. Therefore, there is a power leverage by which those who spend themselves the least in labor are able to bargain away even the barest necessities of life from those who spend themselves totally in lifelong back-breaking, head-splitting, lung-rotting, soul-destroying drudgery in inhuman conditions for work hours that stretch far beyond utter exhaustion and far beyond any possibility of rational or creative projection of human alternatives.

To this, many Christians will quickly respond that the situation is regrettable but that they themselves are not guilty of creating it, are not in a position to change it, and moreover are so far from being rich themselves that they can scarcely make ends meet. The doctrine of original sin is there, however, to remind us that we have the responsibility to cope with many problems of which we are not personally guilty. Not to take an oppositional stance is to become an accomplice in the sinful state of affairs. Individuals as individuals cannot change the whole tenor of society but they can join or even initiate groups and movements that have enough leverage on legislation, on investment and consumption patterns, on public policy in housing or taxation or foreign trade agreements, to change things. It may not be possible to bring about a big change or an immediate change but that scarcely absolves us from changing what we can.

Most middle income people of the wealthy nations today feel that they can scarcely make ends meet. This is partly because inflation, increasing taxation due largely to defense and armaments expenditures, and the pressure on space for city living accommodations (among other factors) create a sense of insecurity and a sense of losing ground all the time. Many well-informed experts have starkly told us that the fact of the matter is: if mankind is to survive at all, we of the wealthy nations must drastically cut our consumption patterns or standard of living—the very advice that the gospel has been giving us from the beginning. The truth is that in our world today those who have any home at all and can also eat are wealthy and called upon to share with those in need. Those who can buy new clothes, can choose food for variety and taste, can afford medical and dental care, and can afford some entertainment are very wealthy indeed and stand at the table of the Eucharist looking like Dives beside Lazarus.

Questions for Discussion

1. Is the concept of blessing entirely strange to our society, or do we know it in some other forms, e.g., Christmas cards, toasts, birthday presents?

2. In what ways have we been particularly blessed by God, and by other people?

3. In what ways are we, as individuals, as a group, as a nation evidently called upon to be a blessing to others?

CHAPTER FIVE

The Eucharist: A Sacrament

Previous chapters have suggested that among the levels of experience and meaning that make up the Eucharist, the most fundamental is that of the sharing of food, which is contained within a fairly elaborate ritual of blessing. But blessing, in turn, does not have a simple or univocal meaning. Rather it has a range of meanings that must be evoked by stories because it cannot be defined in an exhaustive or precise way. As the meaning of blessing is built up by stories and images, we approach the understanding of Eucharist that has been most explicit in Christian tradition, that of Eucharist as sacrament.

The Eucharist is the assembling of people for an action. That action is supposed to make a difference, to bring about a change. Here again, it is certainly of crucial importance how we understand the change that it is supposed to effect. Most Catholics are used to the explanation that a sacrament is a sign that gives grace. In a more explicit form, the teaching of the church is that those actions that we call sacraments are outward or visible signs (happenings accessible to experience) of inward or hidden grace (the openness to God that brings about a gradual but pervasive transformation of all human affairs), signs which not only point to that pervasive transforming quality of being, but also help to bring it about because they are in a true sense the actions of Jesus himself. This is quite an important and helpful definition. The Eucharist is the principal sacrament within this definition, at least if we are speaking of distinct and particular actions. (Contemporary theology has pointed out that in a broader sense the church itself in all its activities is a sacrament, and that the person of Jesus in history is even more fundamentally the sacrament of the transformation of the world in grace.)

Frequently the formula that defines sacrament is used without much reflection on its meaning. The danger is that quietly, implicitly, a meaning may be understood which would never be accepted if it were explicitly discussed. The understanding of the Eucharist among Christians has suffered from this. We have sometimes spoken and acted as though the Eucharist had meaning in isolation from the rest of life—as though participation in it guarantees growth in grace independently of the manner in which the participants live their lives in the world. Yet people who participate reverently and frequently in the Eucharist but drive hard bargains against the weak, taking advantage of the misfortunes of others to enrich themselves, or preferring the aesthetic pleasure of a "devout" and serene private life untroubled by the annoyance and struggle of social justice issues, are confronted by the prophetic denunciations of both Testaments, which declare there can be no growth in intimacy with God except by allowing one's life to be disrupted rudely and painfully by the needs of others. As we know from the parable of the Good Samaritan, Jesus understood "others" not in terms of relatives or fellow community members, but in universal or potentially universal terms. In this parable the other is the one whose need is placed before me. In the parable of Dives and Lazarus, the other is the one who was not even noticed because his suffering was part of the situation that was taken for granted, because his suffering simply blended into a serene world where everything was in its appointed place. Dives is punished, not for turning down an appeal for help, but for not knowing there had ever been any need.

The definition of sacrament, when not carefully considered, may suggest that grace is some sort of substance, stored by God and bestowed by him on those who do what they have been told to do to earn it. But grace is not a substance. It is a relationship with God and with his creation. As such it is not something that can be handled or seen, but it can be seen in its operation or effects. Another way of speaking about the relationship with God, which we call grace, is to speak of charity. Charity can be seen in its operation, and that operation is concern for, and commitment to, the needs of others. There can of course be love and concern over one's own children to the exclusion of others, one's own race or nation to the exclusion of others, and so on. But divine charity, that sharing in God's own love, which is also meant by the relationship we call grace, is by nature non-exclusive. It is practiced (expressed, exercised) by openness to the unexpected, the hitherto unseen demands of others' needs, to those that are beyond the acceptable boundaries of the society and culture—the stranger, the unworthy, the one without civil rights, the one belonging to a nation or people "which does not count," "which is not quite like us," "which does not really expect what we do," "which is used to starvation, poverty, continuous war," and so on. If the love of God cannot be authentic unless expressed in love of neighbor, and if the love of neighbor (to be a sharing in the divine love) must be non-exclusive, and if charity and grace are different ways of speaking about the same thing, then there is no such thing as a growth in grace through participation in the Eucharist where this is isolated from a lifestyle which is a progressive awareness and concern for the suffering of all the oppressed.

In fact, this is the way in which the *Constitution on the Liturgy* of Vatican II looks at the Eucharist. It is discussed as the summit or peak of Christian life to which all things must lead and from which all must flow. In other words, a profound change is intended and expected, which has to do with the totality of human life, in all its aspects both public and private. The entrance into the death of Jesus and his Resurrection in a common celebration with others not only leads to a deepening of experience, but also involves a declaration or public commitment to an oppositional stance in the world. It involves acceptance and assimilation of values radically in opposition to the respectable and established patterns of the world.

Even as it stands, then, the customary definition of sacrament is really more far-reaching and far more exigent than is often acknowledged. However, an interesting point is made by a contemporary Jewish scholar, Eric C. Werner, a student of the liturgies of various traditions. He maintains that the customary Catholic definition of sacrament omits an element that seems to be demanded by the biblical background to the Christian sacraments, namely, covenant. A sacrament is always an act that establishes a covenant community. This seems to be important and true to experience. Whether we are aware of it or not, Eucharist constitutes the church. And the church in turn is the community of people who have entered explicitly, consciously, into the renewed covenant of the death of Jesus. Eucharist constitutes the church, historically, because in the early centuries it quite clearly concluded the initiation of members; those who participated were full members, and those who were not full members were excluded. It constitutes the church, also, because it is in the celebration of the Eucharist (especially the Sunday Eucharist) that the community assembles explicitly to be church. It is in that Sunday assembly that they identify themselves to one another as members of a Christian community, and there is an inevitable element of commitment in this "standing up to be counted." Therefore, in the continued celebrations, the covenant community that is church is constantly being formed anew.

But if this is a fundamental aspect of sacrament, then it is also important to ask what we mean by covenant and what we mean by this renewed covenant in the death of Jesus. The notion of covenant and the Hebrew word for it are drawn from ancient customs of tribal and political alliance: "Your cause shall be my cause, your enemies my enemies, your friends my friends." There can, of course, be only one covenant between God and mankind—the covenant that is built into creation itself, the covenant that is made with the family of mankind. But there are different ways that individual persons and whole peoples can be invited into that one universal covenant. There is ultimately only one covenant because God is One and God does not fight against God, because God as Redeemer does not contradict God as Creator. There are many ways that human persons are invited into the one covenant, because while God is simple, mankind and its history are extremely complex. The covenantal relationship is not simply predetermined and foreordained by God, it is shaped and conditioned by the freedom of persons. This in turn is a conditioned or situated freedom shaped by the consequences of other persons' actions.

Thus, biblically, we recognize a covenant implicit in the very pattern of creation, a covenant known in various ways to all persons through their own experience of existence, through the various hungers that make up their being, and through the satisfactions that those hungers find. But this is a covenant, not between each individual person and God; it is a covenant between mankind and God. The bond with God is interdependent with the community of mankind. It is only as a community that mankind is able to enter into relationship with God, because it is only in community that any relationship becomes possible, and it is only by relationships that a person is constituted. When we think of all that belongs particularly to being human—thinking, speaking, laughing, weeping, planning ahead, making critical assessments, inventing things and new ways, and so on—it becomes clear how much all human becoming depends on relationships with others, on the support and encouragement and challenge that they give, on their example and their willingness to pass on accumulated wisdom.

But people often have very little experience of covenantal relationship with God, because their hungers are left unfulfilled, their hopes cheated by other persons, in a world of human affairs that is out of focus, out of tune in its values and expectations. This is why people are always searching for a redemptive community, a new covenant community that will set things right. Ancient times had mystery religions, secret societies of initiates and such like. Today we have encounter groups and other such phenomena. The bible gives us one classic story, which is really a story about many new beginnings among different peoples and at different times, in the present and the future as well as in the past. It is the story of Noah. The world is so wicked that it is inundated again by a new on-rush of the great destructive primeval waters of chaos. An up-right, morally sensitive person is sufficiently in tune with God to see the destruction coming, and gathers a small, like-minded family into a close community of a quite different life style, supporting one another in a new beginning. The waters of de-struction allow this new community to survive and it finds it-self confirmed in a new (or rather renewed) covenant with God, a covenant made explicit in terms of a moral basis for the community. It is a story in which we have probably all taken part. It is a story that accounts for many religious and ethical movements entirely outside the historical boundaries of the Jewish and Christian influences.

Beyond this the bible gives us a series of covenantal sto-ries concerned with the people and land of Israel from Abra-ham to Sinai. We are told that God makes a solemn covenant with Abraham, the patriarch, to bless him in his descendants, so that through them all the peoples of the earth will be blessed. This clearly intends a special participation in the universal cov-enant—a privileged participation. But it is a privilege for oth-ers. Immediately after the promise stories, we are given a se-quel that is one of the great classic paradoxes of all history. Abraham hears a call to bind his only son upon the altar of sacrifice to be slain. Christian accounts of this story are in-clined to move quickly through this phase and emphasize the angel's staying hand and the ram in the bushes found as a sub-stitute. This is unfortunate because it evades the point of the story that is a very important one for our understanding of the covenant into which we also claim to be called. Jews do not move through this story quickly to its conclusion because they know that this is not only a story of prehistoric or very early historic times. This is a story about the Jews of all ages—a story about the sufferings of the Jews under the Inquisition, a story about the death of the six million in our own times in the

Nazi holocaust, a story about the Jews of Russia and Iraq in recent times, a story about all Jews. The victims of the holocaust died a fearful death because their great grandparents in fidelity to the covenant of Abraham (the covenant of circumcision) had in effect bound their descendants for several generations to the altar of sacrifice simply by making them socially identifiable as Jews. But the story has even wider significance. The Apostle Paul, himself a Jew passionately interested in Jewish tradition and identity, nevertheless insists that the figure of Abraham in the Hebrew scriptures represents not only the Jews but all believers in the One God. (See, for instance, the Letter to the Galatians, Chapter 3.) To enter into a covenant with God in faith and hope, in an oppositional stance to the values of the world, is always to put not only oneself but one's children at risk.

The story of the calling of Abraham is not complete until the Moses stories are told—the stories of the fashioning of a people in response to the call of God out of slavery into freedom, and out of brutalized self-centeredness into authentic peoplehood. This is not a new or different covenant, but it is an invitation into a very intimate sharing of the covenant of God with mankind. It is an invitation to make a fresh start as a very explicit and conscious covenant community, by taking root in a certain land—not a rich or fertile land comparatively speaking, but central—and constructing there a people all of whose affairs would be governed by a fundamental orientation to the One God.

Such a covenant people is not blessed at the expense of others. The blessing is received by becoming a blessing for others. Infidelity in this response of being a blessing for others does not end the covenant but turns it into a heavy burden, This is why we have the stories of the exiles and captivities and conquests. It would be easy to read the bible thinking of God as vindictive, swift to fall upon offenders to punish them, getting angry as a person might and wanting revenge. Yet, we may understand our relation to God better by thinking for a moment in practical, human, even non-religious terms. When one person in a group, one child in a family, one district of a country, one nation among its neighbors is in some way particularly blessed or rightly endowed and enjoys that endowment so that benefits accrue to the others, then the privileged one is secure because the blessing received has become a blessing for others. But when one singled out by a special blessing hoards the advantage, lords it over others, boasts of it, uses it against others to oppress them, then the blessing turns into something more like a curse because it arouses envy and anger over the oppression. All of this can be understood simply on practical human terms without attributing vengeful behavior to God.

In the whole history of mankind it has been difficult not only for the people of Israel, the Jews, but for all who have enjoyed a special blessing to appreciate that all blessings are given so as to become a blessing for others. It has been difficult always and for all persons and groups to understand that there can be no special covenant with God that is exclusive of others' well-being; there can only be a special participation in the one universal covenant with God, which is with all mankind. Therefore, any special participation is always a privilege for the benefit not only of the holder but of others through this special covenant partner. The reason for writing about this in covenant terms, as suggested by the Jewish scholar mentioned above, is that it brings out in a more vivid way the meaning of our eucharistic communities.

Christians have always claimed that in the person of Jesus, and more particularly in the death of Jesus, we have a new and universal covenant. This has sometimes been understood as though it were a new and different covenant that outdated the old. As explained above, that is not a valid interpretation because fundamentally there can only be one covenant between God and mankind and because God does not contradict himself. The most fundamental quality that human reflection discerns in God is fidelity, total reliability, absolute trustworthiness. Therefore, when Christians speak of a new covenant in the blood of Jesus, it has reference to a renewal and a new intimacy or intensity of participation in the same great universal covenant. It also has reference to a breakthrough into universal dimensions.

In the gospel according to Matthew we hear Jesus early in the Sermon on the Mount, insisting that his mission and intent is not to abrogate the law and the prophets but to fulfill them because it is impossible that any part of the covenant be set aside. It is not to be cancelled out but brought to completion. And this is precisely what Christians see in Jesus. They see him seizing the heritage of his people, the law, the prophets, the traditions of prayer and observance, and always penetrating to the heart and kernel of it. His words are radical and bold, but so is his life and the life into which he initiates the small circle of disciples that gathers around him. From him they learn to distinguish what lies at the heart of the covenant and what is simply supporting structure for it. It would not be true to suppose that the other Jews of the time of Jesus were blinded (any more than human communities at any other time or place) or that they had not been able to discern the heart of the law and the tradition until he came. The gospels tell us the contrary with the story of the lawyer who asks Jesus what is the greatest commandment. In that story Jesus turns the question back to him and he gives the answer that Jesus approves: to inherit eternal life the essential thing that one must do is to love God with one's whole heart and soul and substance, and one's neighbor as oneself. The story is told somewhat variantly by the three evangelists, Matthew, Mark and Luke. But they are agreed that Jesus embarrassed people who were trying to embarrass him by showing them how obvious the answer to the question was. It was an answer that was already known and appreciated. But people then, as now, do not easily accept such a simple answer because such a simple answer is too demanding. It does not easily permit of loopholes. Hence the follow-up question about who the neighbor might be. What we usually translate "with all your strength" in this text probably has reference to substance, goods, possessions. Then, as now, it was hard, especially for relatively rich people, to admit that God and the needy neighbor had a claim on the whole of one's goods—that everything was only held in stewardship and was therefore a blessing received for others.

The gospels give us this as an indication of the ways in which Jesus went straight to the heart of the matter, discerning with ruthless clarity the patterns of sin and selfishness and the causes of human suffering. The gospels also give us many stories about the scandal that people of his own time and nation took from Jesus because he seemed so unconcerned with the question of getting the Roman forces of occupation out of the country. Jesus seemed to be saying that the leadership within the country was corrupt, the morale of the whole people low, the rich and powerful constantly taking advantage of the poor and powerless, so that the much more urgent change to loosen the bonds of sin and servitude was the change that had to be brought about within the people. The liberation of the people had to begin with a very radical and organic change in the quality of life and the quality of relationships among people. That is what he called for—a covenant renewal, which would be a rediscovery of peoplehood and at the same time a rediscovery of intimacy with God. But peoplehood, or community, consists in subordinating one's own, or family, or partisan welfare to that of the whole community. This requires very deep trust both in God and in other persons. Within the sinful pattern of human dealings in the world, we have all learned to trust rather in armaments and fortifications, in accumulation of goods and power over others, than to trust in others. Then, as now, people were convinced they were more likely to survive by excluding than by including others, by dominating rather than by befriending them. Then, as now, this was true not only of the Roman conqueror but also of the oppressed people in their relations with one another.

In many ways, Jesus found a social and political situation that was quite closely akin to the social and political situation that Moses found among the Hebrews. The gospels show him wrestling in prayer with the problems of human frustration and despair and suffering all around him, and in the story of the forty days in the desert we see him rejecting as false three ways of salvation proposed to him by the tempter, Satan. There emerges in the accounts of the public ministry, a new picture of the covenant of God with mankind and a new perspective as to how one enters into it. Clearly the manner of the public ministry of Jesus suggests that he saw the covenant people of God built up from below by small face to face communities learning to live in a totally different pattern of relationships with one another—learning this from his presence among them, his friendship and his style of life. He evidently saw no possibility of building up the covenant people to respond to God by organizing them from above, for instance, by liberating them from the Roman occupation and then setting a new government over them. This seems to have been what some or many of his most ardent followers were hoping he would do, even up to the time of his death. The gospels more than suggest that this was the great scandal to Judas and to those of the Zealot party who might well have joined forces with him.

The gospels suggest that Jesus found it easier to work among the poorer or the more oppressed or despised people. Perhaps they were more aware of their needs—of their unfilled or cheated hungers. Again and again the rich and powerful fail to understand what he is about or how his way of life and community will change anything for the better. In fact, he tends to be seen as a threat to those well on the way to enriching themselves or strengthening their positions of power. They are afraid to trust him. He has to begin to build his community with those who have absolutely no possibility of trusting in accumulation of goods or power, for the simple reason that they have no opportunity to accumulate any. In their desperation, with no protection against cruelty and destruction, they are ready to listen to Jesus, though perhaps from motives that are less than sublime. Even to them his message of sharing, of non-violence, of ultimate generosity and self-gift, of trust in love rather than power, seems a hard saying, and we see them repeatedly looking for some sort of magic to give more force to God's covenant with them.

We know today how it ended. The personal freedom of the listeners and followers of Jesus was so small, the task of creatively loving them into a more secure personal stance from which they could authentically love others was so great, that the forces of evil marshalled themselves to condemn and eliminate Jesus from the scene, when he had been able to do for his followers so much less than he desired. They were still oriented to receive rather than to give, to be defended and encouraged rather than to defend and encourage others. Jesus knew that the end was coming, and having loved into life and creativity those who had come to him, there was nothing else he could do but to love them to the limits of his life and personhood, even to the point of his own destruction, and then to surrender his spirit and his unfinished task to the Father and to them, his followers.

To sustain their being and their full personhood, so that they might in turn sustain the life and being and personhood of others, Jesus gave them himself as their sustenance. And to give them himself meant to give them his death—his premature death by torture and public political execution. More than that no one can give. And it is in this light, of course, that we must see the total picture of the Christian claim of the new (renewed) covenant. It is in this light that we must understand the Eucharist as sacrament, as sign of the covenant, constituting the covenant community.

On the eve of his passion and death, Jesus gathers the small inner circle of his companions and followers and invites them to celebrate the Passover seder with him. As mentioned in an earlier chapter, it was certainly not the first time he celebrated it with them, but it was the most solemn time. Taking the elements and blessings that belong to the traditional celebration, he expounds their meaning (as the presiding person at the table is supposed to do). But he expounds their meaning with referencc to the present and the future of those around the table and of all mankind. He attempts to explain to them the meaning of his death by inserting the tragedy that is about to occur in his and their lives within the Passover meditation on suffering and liberation and the wonderful works of God in history. He offers them the unleavened bread, known as the bread of affliction from the Exodus story, where the Hebrews were so hard pressed they could not even wait to leaven the dough. And he explains what is this bread of affliction, which is also the bread of freedom, of the passing over into a new life. That bread of affliction is his person, his presence among them, his body to be broken for the redemption of the world. In the same way he offers them the cup of blessing, a cup of wine, life-blood of the grape, and explains the ancient theme of passing over from death to life with the new meaning of his own death for them and through them for the vast hosts of mankind.

It is in this context that Jesus invites his disciples to eat and drink with him. This is not like the multiplication of the loaves when all who were there and were hungry were fed. At the multiplication of the loaves there was not, as far as we know, any particular commitment on the part of those who took food other than that they had continued to follow him to hear what he had to say. At the Last Supper Jesus makes it quite clear that to eat and drink of the unleavened bread and the cup of blessing is to enter into intimate fellowship with him in his death—to accept what he does for them and to do this for others. In fact, later, most of those who had sat around that table gave up their own lives in order to proclaim his message and eventually suffered death by torture and execution. What Jesus did at this meal, then, was indeed to establish a covenant community. He established a covenant among them because of the bond that they had solemnly ratified on this occasion with him. That bond with him drew them in a new and intimate way into the great covenant of God with all mankind. That covenant had been specified in Abraham and in the leadership of Moses and was now specified in a new way in him, Jesus. It was sealed in his death.

There has been much theologizing as to how we of later generations fit into this action. From what has been said so far it should be clear that there is much more than a memorial at stake. We are invited as they were invited to share in an action that has momentous consequences. As Paul wrote in his First Letter to the Corinthians, we may not participate lightly but have to ask ourselves whether we really intend what is meant by the eating and drinking of the eucharistic banquet—whether we really mean that we accept the gift that Jesus makes us of himself in his death, knowing that the acceptance of it means a radically different way of life and of relating to all other people. It means this because a new life, a radically changed way of life is the content of the gift that Jesus bestows on his followers. Not only our first, but every participation in the Eucharist is an encounter with Jesus demanding a radical decision to commit oneself or to withhold oneself from the covenant community which must be a transformed community engaged in the redemptive task of Jesus in the world.

All this has become very much obscured in the course of time, because for many centuries all the externals of the Christian community have become part of the cultural heritage for most peoples of the Western world. In other words, for many centuries, church communities (with the exception of the Anabaptist churches) have been composed largely of people who had never been called upon for a personal option. Most parishioners had been raised in Christian families, taken to church, given religious instruction, had sacraments "conferred upon" them, and had always been called, and identified themselves as, Christians. Relatively few Christians have searched into the meaning of the heritage and discovered that to be a Christian is really a far-reaching and quite drastic commitment, placing oneself in stark opposition to many of the values taken for granted even in Christian countries. Most Christians have assumed that unless a government declared itself as atheistic or anti-religious, its policies and its economic structures must be basically moral. Only the Christians of the Anabaptist churches have taken it for granted that to be a Christian is to be called on for civil disobedience and protest quite frequently. Yet to enter through the Eucharist into the covenant is to accept far more seriously the brotherhood, the common destiny of mankind, and the obligations toward the needy among all mankind than any state has ever been willing to do.

Questions for Discussion

1. What is your understanding of "sacrament," and how has this understanding developed as you matured?
2. Does the concept of "covenant" make sense in our lives today?
3. Is the idea of Jesus and church as sacraments a new one?

CHAPTER SIX

Sacrifice and Transformation

We are quite accustomed, at least in Catholic circles, to hearing the Eucharist described in terms of sacrifice, but it is a term that bears some reflection and examination. There have been some ways of speaking of the sacrifice of Jesus and the sacrifice of the Eucharist that might mislead us into thinking that we are speaking here simply of something that happened to Jesus whereby our prospects for the future are changed, without anything ever happening that changes us. This would be quite false.

Because the word and the notion of sacrifice are common to the traditions of many peoples, they contain a great deal of ambiguity. The New Testament writers interpret the death of Jesus as a sacrifice, strictly in the biblical tradition and with the biblical connotations. In the three synoptic gospels of Matthew, Mark and Luke, Jesus is reported to have made the identification himself in the blessing over the cup, which the eucharistic canon of the Catholic liturgy has kept in the same form: "This is the cup of my blood, of the new and everlasting covenant, that is to be shed for you and for the many." The First Letter to the Corinthians goes further by an explicit comparison or contrast between the meaning of the participation in the Eucharist and the participation in the eating of meat that has been sacrificed to idols (or in any other act of idol worship). The Letter to the Hebrews works out a whole theology of sacrifice in relation to the cross of Jesus, comparing it to the many sacrifices offered in the Temple, which had never achieved their purpose.

The Hebrew understanding of sacrifice that provides the context for these passages is one of "making holy," of crossing over into the realm of the holy, of coming into a share of the divine life. If death was part of the act of sacrifice, that was not in order to destroy but in order to cross over into the realm of God. If eating was part of the sacrifice, that was in order to become one with God into whose realm the offering had crossed over.

All of this is actually much easier to understand with reference to Jesus and the Eucharist than it is to understand it with reference to animal or cereal sacrifices. A ritual enactment of sending an animal to cross over and then participating in a covenant meal with God to whom the slaughtered animal now belongs, is a powerful symbolic expression of the worshipping assembly's longing for union with God. However, it does not add much to what the same community could do simply by praying, because the animal, of course, cannot be a mediator, so the alienation between the worshippers and God is acknowledged but not bridged. Any difference in their position is really not made by the sacrifice but by their own prayer and conversion of hearts.

When the death of Jesus is presented as a sacrifice, a quite different dimension is introduced. He was slain, as the Holy Week liturgy insistently reminds us, because he himself willed it. This was in the most unique way a genuine crossing over into the realm of the Holy God. That is why the Letter to the Hebrews presents us with the image of Jesus as both priest and victim of the sacrifice, because he "offers his own body," that is, makes the crossing in his own person. But he makes the crossing not just because he dies, but because of the motive and meaning of his death. He goes into death because he will not compromise in doing the Father's will. Looked at from his enemies' point of view, he goes into death because he does not fit into their world and they cannot tolerate him in their world and have to push him out of it totally and irrevocably. He is literally thrust out of the sinful world into God's realm where he belongs. In a more profound sense presented to us in the gospel of John, he enters by his death into the divine realm from which he can indeed send his spirit into his followers.

A man while he lives is not yet pure creative love as God is; he is simply bound to be in some sense self-assertion over against others. A man while he lives occupies a space physically and socially and psychologically, which cannot then be occupied by another; he speaks a challenge which is spoken to the other and not within him; he exists side by side and over against others and is therefore necessarily in some sense a rival and a threat. Though sinless, Jesus could not be other than this until he crossed over through death to be as God is and act as God acts. But when Jesus crosses over something has really changed, definitively, radically. The depth of human experience—of human suffering, humiliation, frustration and longing—is brought into the creative and redemptive love of God.

The meaning of the Resurrection is that the crossing over is confirmed. Those who were attuned to him soon learned that his enemies could not really push him out of their world, that he lived in that same world in a new and more pervasive way, and that all power in heaven and on earth was now given to him to redeem the world in and through his followers. Now he was able to breathe on them the Spirit that was his spirit, uniting him with the Father, that it might become their Spirit uniting them with him and the Father, to be one as he and the Father were and ever are one. That oneness is the oneness of total presence to others, total blessing to others, total self-gift, not needing to assert oneself over against the other, or protect one's interests at the expense of the other.

When we celebrate Eucharist, we do indeed participate in the sacrifice of Jesus. We are summoned again to be present at the moment of his entering into death (but now also at the moment that includes the Resurrection). We are summoned to be as present as we can at that moment—and more present than we can. We are called to become one with his crossing over and to eat of the sacrificial banquet in order to participate in the life of Jesus who is now "on the other side," on God's side, on the side of self-gift rather than self-assertion, on the side of total community and total sharing, on the side of creative love.

To the extent that we are open to receive the gift of himself that Jesus offers in the Eucharist, we are indeed able to live now the divine life. But that divine life is characterized not by absence of effort or temptation or problems; it is characterized by one quality: creative love.

It is this creative love that erupts out of the resurrection of the crucified Jesus that is able to make fresh beginnings in situations that have soured long ago. It is such a creative love that can begin to work from the bottom up and permeate a society like leaven, gradually altering the quality of human relationships and of human life, from desperate self-assertion, self-aggrandizement, self-defense to empathy, compassion and concern to fill the needs of others which lead to progressive self-forgetfulness and perhaps even ecstasy. It is through this creative love that grace itself becomes experiential. This is why the term in the New Testament always corresponds to qualities discerned in the believing communities—qualities that were even evident to unbelievers.

The Eucharist is indeed a sacrifice. It is the sacrifice of Jesus in his death made present so that we can enter into it again in our present situation and with our experience. But it cannot be this without also being the sacrifice of the covenant community that gathers to celebrate. The community as such and the individual persons in that community must, to the extent that they enter into the action, become themselves a sacrifice and a bridge by which others are able to cross over to share in the divine life. This is why the early church related the stories of the martyrs in eucharistic language. Evidently those who witnessed their deaths were conscious of having been present at a moment of covenant grace, bridging the alienation of man from God—a moment which in some sense was identical with the moment of Christ's crossing over, just as in some sense every eucharistic celebration is identical with Christ's moment of crossing over.

Martyrdom soon became the prototype or exemplar of the Christian life. The radical totality of the self-gift of the martyr became the model for the Christian life, described as one of death to self. But it is worthwhile to reflect carefully on what Christians of the past meant by death to self. They certainly did not mean suicide, either in a physical biological sense or in a psychological sense of abandonment of social or personal responsibilities and decision making, or critical awareness and intellectual effort. Clearly they meant death to self-seeking, self-assertion, death to the old worldly way of living in order to cross over into a new life of community with others in Christ.

But this kind of community and this kind of crossing over into new life cannot be institutionally guaranteed. This is something that must be begun over and over again, by new conversions, even in the community of those already committed by personal decision. This is why we celebrate Eucharist frequently. This is also why we read the scriptures in our eucharistic celebration and (whenever possible) have a homily preached to interpret the scriptures in our present situation. We cannot ever assume that the demands of creative love are clear and spelled out, or that we understand what the death of Jesus means in any depth. One cannot really know what the Eucharist means until one has really died so that others may have life. But while we have not yet died we must nevertheless keep tuning in to the word of God in our midst, trying to understand the mystery of which we are called to be a part.

This kind of tuning in means more, of course, than sitting in the pew and hearing words spoken. One can only tune in with one's whole life style. The simplest beginning is the willingness to share material things with the needy—the willingness to let the needs of the oppressed of the world be expressed, even if the demands are overwhelming and depressing and cannot be met. The eucharistic gathering is of all places the most suitable place for the cry of the oppressed to be uttered and considered. Jesus crucified is above all representative of the marginated, despised and oppressed, of those who "don't count" and are kept out of sight (socially invisible), of those who are outsiders and have no rights. It is not possible to be one with Jesus in the moment of his death and yet ignore the poor and suffering of the world. It is not possible to cross over in the sacrifice of the death of Jesus into the life of God, and to leave behind the poor and the oppressed of the world. To accept the bread of the Eucharist is to accept to be bread and sustenance for the poor of the world.

Having followed the chapters concerning the Eucharist as blessing, sacrament and sacrifice, some Catholic readers may well wonder why there has still not been any mention of transubstantiation as the main theological explanation of the meaning of the Eucharist. In fact all these three chapters have been concerned with transubstantiation, but have approached the topic from a very different perspective than may have been expected. The Eucharist is a mystery of God's grace and mankind's salvation, and transubstantiation is a word which our tradition has used as a reference to that mystery. Like all religious language, this word is a hint about something we cannot comprehend because it is much too great and because it lies at the boundary of what human language is competent to express at all. The only way we can really approach the meaning of such mysteries and such words is by stories and images that evoke answering echoes in our own experience and which expand that experience by building bridges of empathy. To suppose we could comprehend such a mystery and give it precise definition and explanation, would be to cut ourselves off from the real challenge to prayer and conversion of life style.

Nevertheless, some important historical points must be made about the word transubstantiation. The early church did speak in terms of a change being effected in the Eucharist, but the reference was first and foremost to the members of the congregation and to the gifts on the altar only instrumentally as they related to the event in which the congregation was transformed. St. Augustine of Hippo did use the very word transubstantiation (along with similar words that all had the sense of a crossing over, and all echoed the biblical notion of sacrifice as discussed here). Augustine discusses the change that must take place in the congregation and the change that takes place on the altar, because we are not there to satisfy bodily hunger but seek for sustenance for our lives in a far more embracing and far-reaching sense. In the medieval schools the theology of the Eucharist was discussed in various ways. For St. Thomas Aquinas the central issue seems to have been the relation between the Resurrection, the Eucharist and the Church, and the manner of Christ's personal presence and action in history. Some authors were very much concerned with a philosophically tenable explanation of the change in the bread and wine. The reason for this seems to have been the rather corrupt liturgical practices of the time, which made it very urgent to explain that we were not dealing with magic. Out of these efforts rose many disputes and problems, and some conciliar definitions that attempted to resolve the disputes. Among other things, these definitions used the word transubstantiation because it seemed one of the safer and more traditional ones, but some thoughtful people have worried over this. The reason is this: when Augustine of Hippo used the word, it was not understood as having any precise philosophical content, but the meaning of words changes over the centuries and this word came later to have rather specific philosophical content. For most people this discussion is academic, but the word transubstantiation may still carry the very connotations it was suppose to correct. Substance suggests a chemical notion, and there may be some inclination to suppose that in the Eucharist we are speaking of a sort of superior meta-chemistry, just a little more inaccessible than the chemistry we learn by laboratory experiments. The trouble in that case is that we are fairly and squarely back into the problem of magical explanations, namely, explanations that bypass any need for personal conversion or change of life styles.

All this having been said, the word transubstantiation represents in Catholic theology the teaching that in the Eucharist it is really Jesus who touches us in our present situation and our present lives, not just the memory but the presence, the power, the death and the challenge. In other words it expresses the teaching that there is more to do than a ceremony in the participation in the Eucharist; there is a total transformation of life and of relating to others.

This makes of the Eucharist both a challenge and a support. Throughout the Christian centuries, the Eucharist has been experienced by saints and mystics and heroes of the tradition, but also by many quite ordinary and unexceptional people, as sustenance in a very real sense. They have experienced it as a source of courage and strength in coping with difficult situations, as a source of inspiration for creative solutions to painful problems, as a steadying guide in maintaining a prayerful focus in their lives, as a kind of door that opens to let them glimpse heaven. In other words, many people have found the Eucharist profoundly satisfying their own many dimensional hungers, and this, of course, it is intended to do. All of us require a certain input of creative love and sustenance for our lives and basic needs before we can reach a "take-off point" of any sort of concern to provide sustenance for others out of our own lives and persons, and all of us are creatures who do not exist or continue to exist at all unless we are sustained in existence.

Yet there is a delicate and important issue here. There are in fact two ways of thinking about the death of Jesus and therefore about the Eucharist. The death of Jesus can be seen in an extreme way as substituting for us, so that we remain (in terms of salvation) forever passive receivers of his grace with no further responsibilities than to acknowledge that we are sinners and receivers of mercy through Jesus. Though generally thought of as a Protestant theological position, this understanding is pervasive in some well-established patterns of Catholic piety in relation to the Eucharist, while at the same time it would never be accepted as Catholic theology. The alternate way of thinking about the death of Jesus is the one that has been suggested, in which Jesus does not substitute for us but initiates something into which we are invited as participants. In this view there is no way of receiving the redemptive grace of Jesus in a purely passive fashion. His grace is received as a changed quality of life, and life is what we live. A changed life has to be expressed in a changed life style, and the key characteristic of that changed life style is not a feeling of exhilaration or serenity, but the serious practice of universal (non-exclusive) charity which is the exercise of the creative love of God. This in turn is a very practical matter, the dimensions of which are only revealed in proportion as a community makes serious efforts to be non-exclusive, that is not to screen out from consideration the needs that are too vast, too compromising, too complex, too overwhelming.

The two ways of understanding the death of Jesus and our call to respond to it might be expressed in another way. The question is whether we are called to enter into the experience of the death of Jesus and his crossing over from death to life by standing opposite him, looking at him, thanking him and meditating on it, or by standing with him, seeing what he sees, trying to embrace what he embraces and taking up the task where he leaves it in his death, knowing that the Spirit that he breathes into us is greater than we are and therefore adequate to the task. Obviously, the response must be both. It would be sheer folly to suppose that one is really ready at any time to do what Jesus did, but it would seem equally to be in contradiction to scripture and tradition to conclude that we are not therefore all called to share in his redemptive work, growing to that mature human personhood that is genuinely able to look outward to others.

Questions for Discussion

1. What images, stories and connections arise spontaneously from the term "sacrifice"?

2. Is it still a useful term in connection with the Eucharist, or does it have too many inappropriate connections?

3. What new insights have been sparked by this chapter concerning the Eucharist and transformation?

CHAPTER SEVEN

Christian Mission to the Hungry of the World

Today there is a great reluctance about the question of mission. On the one hand we remember the mandate of Jesus to go and teach all nations and the conviction of the church since earliest times that the gospel is good news not only for us but for all mankind and that we must therefore go and tell it. But on the other hand we look at the world today and we reconsider the history of Christian missions, realizing how much harm was done as well as good. We look also at the other religions of the world and see so much in them that is obviously of God and which grows so naturally and harmoniously out of the cultures of the people. We are no longer confident that we are in secure possession of all the good news and that the others are in the dark from which we must rescue them.

The question constantly arises whether there is scope for missionary activity and what form it should take. Perhaps the problems arise largely because we have assumed that to bring the good news means to speak words, and that the purpose of speaking those words can only be to invite people to learn our doctrines in our words, make a profession of faith in those words, and then participate in the worship activities of our church. Perhaps our understanding of good news is too narrow. In the Last Supper discourse of St. John's Gospel we have the injunction of Jesus to love one another as he has loved us so that the world may know that the Father has sent him.

As mentioned in an earlier chapter, the world is hungry with many hungers and, for the most part, with obviously unfulfilled hungers. Mankind knows, though perhaps in an inchoate, inarticulate sort of way, the need of redemption. Those who suffer physically from the greed and fear and domination of others know it best and most urgently. The words of Jesus seem to suggest that those who know existentially the need for redemption will also know how to recognize it when authentically redemptive events happen in their midst. This does not apply in the same way to those of us whose needs are met at a physical level and who are on the whole so comfortable that we are not really aware that we are in serious need of redemption. But Jesus himself found that those most frequently open to his person and his message were the most oppressed. Moreover his public ministry is described in terms of immediate and effective compassion for the physical sufferings of the people.

Good news is communicated by what we are and how we relate to others. It is communicated by our total life style and our concerns. It is communicated by the real difference that we make in the situation. The words that may be spoken have very little to do with the communication of the good news. To say, "Cheer up, Jesus loves you," is very different from listening to someone with interest who has not often before been taken seriously. To say "God will provide" is sheer nonsense when spoken by a well-fed person to those who are hungry and watch their children go hungry without being able to do anything about it.

To preach that the salvation of God has come into the world in the person of Jesus, the one and only thing that is necessary is that a community that lives the new life of the Resurrection should touch the lives of the hungry of the world with authentic and generous compassion, drawing on the bread of life that is Jesus, to become themselves bread of life for the needy with their whole heart and their whole mind and their whole substance. Such a community need not even go to the ends of the earth, for in our times the ends of the earth come to us all the time in our newspapers, our mailboxes, our television screens.

Such a community need only be a parish that never says no to an appeal; what begins as a stream of requests for money will certainly develop into a further involvement calling for empathy, compassion, growth in understanding, deeper identification with the oppressed, championing of their cause in public as well as private action. Such a community need only be a group of families or individuals seriously concerned with one social injustice anywhere in the world—racial discrimination, exclusion of a minority, abandonment of the aged or any other man-made suffering. To identify with the oppressed concretely in even one respect and follow through with effective action requires all the resources of a generous and selfless community because it leads into involvement with the whole highly resistant network of sin and selfishness. But where there is any action of creative love, there the good news is preached that salvation has come into the world, and that there is an alternative to desperate self-assertion and self-defense at the expense of others—that there is a possibility of human community.

The reason for calling this mission and preaching of the good news may not immediately be clear. The person and life and death of Jesus reveal to us: first, what it is to be truly human and how very far we are from being truly human; secondly, the creative and redemptive love of God that powerfully calls us to the fulfillment of our human possibilities; and thirdly, the vast and deeply rooted and elaborately entangled consequences of sin that hold individuals and societies back from responding to the call to become truly human. Frequently we cannot even see the alternate possibilities in a situation, because we are cramped by fear, prejudices and greed, or envy or jealousy. A kind of built-in safety monitor makes sure that some options are not even seen. The only way they will ever be seen is through a living community that has actually realized those possibilities. The only way there can be any "de-escalation" of the mutual hostilities of self-aggrandizement, one-upmanship, and frantic acquisition of resources from which others can be excluded, is when someone begins and provides a margin of freedom and safety for others. What we believe is that Jesus has made a definitive and universally valid beginning, and that the community of believers is graced and gifted by his death to enter into his risen life and live themselves an utterly new life style. It is certainly of no use to rush to the ends of the earth to talk to people about this if those who go out as missionaries are not able to speak out of the experience of a community that authentically lives like this. In such a case it is more effective missionary action to begin in whatever way possible and with whomever possible to build such a community with such relations.

This kind of work of building a genuinely Christian community by the joint efforts of people who are trying to convert themselves not others, in life style and not in the words of their allegiance, seems so much less significant and effective than preaching to large crowds and soliciting candidates for baptism. Yet this is really what Jesus did with his disciples, and it is from them and not from the large crowds of five thousand or more that his work continued. Moreover, this would seem to be the true mission in any culture or society and at any time. There is no lack of respect for the culture and tradition of others in such a mission. Salvation in Christ is quietly self-validating so that those who come and seek membership in the community do it from the depth of their own human freedom in response to God calling. But such a mission also certainly proceeds from a celebration of Eucharist that is the summit of life, in the sense that all things lead up to it and all things flow from it in the lives of the participants.

What we learn from the Eucharist when we reflect on its meaning in the context of scripture and tradition and in the light of our own human experience is that the Christian mission to the hungry is to enter into their need and find ways to satisfy their hunger, to challenge the structures of the world that keep some peoples and some populations hungry, to question the sick and inordinate desires that maintain those structures. In other words, the Christian mission to the hungry is to discern the substitute satisfactions that lead those of us in the wealthier nations to entrenched positions from which we cannot even see or hear the cries of the distressed. This in turn means the need to discern the real hungers behind the substitute satisfactions—the hunger for meaning in life, for appreciation and encouragement, for security, for beauty and goodness and truth, the hunger to be needed and have a task to do, the hunger for true human companionship and sharing of interests, and so on.

It is true in one sense that those who are lonely, unloved, unappreciated but rich and possessive about their wealth are as much in need of compassion as those who are poor and physically in want. But it is also true that the solution of their problem is to be brought to do things for others, to share, to surrender what is hoarded, to take risks, to give. The important question is how this is done. The answer cannot be a universal prescription. The answer must be evolved out of a community of creative (challenging and affirming) love. What we know from the gospel accounts of Jesus is that such love is not bland and non-conflictual, yet it cannot be such as to exclude the possibility of a conversion of lifestyle either. A person backed against the wall cannot turn. A person who frantically enriches himself and hoards wealth because he feels insecure will not change his lifestyle if made to feel even less secure (and this describes more or less accurately more less all of us in the middle or upper income brackets in the churches of the Western world today).

What we must draw from the Eucharist and bring to the Eucharist week by week and year by year is the ongoing effort to build authentically Christian grass roots communities in which there is a sufficient level of mutual acceptance and creative love that there can be a discernment in Christ of the roots of our own insecurities and a constant adjustment to a more human and more generous lifestyle. But this is not likely to happen unless the needs of the poorest and the most oppressed are constantly being voiced among us to challenge us and reveal the state of sin and selfishness in which we live and the desperate urgency of conversion not only of individuals but of the values and policies of the great power groups of the world. There is need for a constant unmasking of the interdependence of the hungers of the world and a constant unmasking of false values and sinful structures that can be invisible to those not suffering physically from them.

In the Eucharist we have an answer to despair about the future of the world: we can still live and bid others live because we are drawn into a covenant with God and all mankind within which to give one's life for others is ultimately to save one's life.

Questions for Discussion

1. Is a mission to the hungry of the world really an essential component of the Christian vocation, or is this stretching a point too far?
2. In what practical ways can ordinary Christians participate in such a mission?
3. Does frugality and simplicity in our personal lives really contribute to a more just and hospitable world?

CHAPTER EIGHT

The Eucharist and World Peace

In the global context of our times, the greatest human hunger of all is the hunger for peace, and it is opportune to reflect on the Eucharist as a response to that hunger. To yearn for peace is to desire life for oneself and for others, to desire the fulness of creaturehood in the enjoyment of God's lavish hospitality in creation without fear or unnecessary suffering or premature mourning. Nothing could be more basic than the desire to live one's allotted life span to the full and be serene in the expectation that others around one will be allowed to do the same.

Living in the wealthier industrial nations of the northern and western parts of the world, many of us have never experienced warfare in our own homelands. Except for those serving in the armed forces, or those travellers caught accidentally in war zones, we think of war as essentially something that happens to other people—to people very different from ourselves. For that reason, unless we have had someone close to us serving and suffering in a war, most of us are not inclined to see peace as one of the most urgent needs and hungers of human beings in our time. Those who have had wars swirling to and fro constantly over their own homes see the matter very differently. There are people of all ages living in our world today who have never at any time of their lives experienced what it is to live a normal existence in a country functioning without fear of mass violence threatening everyone's life and physical integrity at every moment of day or night. It is clear enough that such is not the intent of the Creator in calling human persons into existence. It is equally clear that the hospitality of God in creation goes out to all peoples alike, and does not intend that some should use others as pawns in a game, as tools for their own purposes, as disposable items in larger calculations.

Because Eucharist is first and foremost the celebration of the divine hospitality made present to us in the person of Jesus, it is an action which addresses every form of inhospitality in our world, confronting it with the image of what might be and ought to be. Jesus as the outreach of divine hospitality is not only the primary hospitality of creation but the further redemptive hospitality of healing grace. At its simplest level of sharing of food, the Eucharist signals that in God's world there is room for all. We are therefore challenged to solve the problems of the world by sharing, not by eliminating people, not by killing. At its higher level of symbolism, pointing to the Paschal Mystery as foreshadowed by the Exodus event, the Eucharist bids us share in celebrating the liberation of the poor, the oppressed and the marginated or excluded because these are in a special way the People of God. Yet sober reflection will show that none are more marginated, oppressed or excluded than those whose lives are considered the necessary price for the attainment of some "greater" good for others who will survive. None are more marginated or personally discounted than conscript soldiers, peasants who are "unfortunately" in the strategic area, people of all ages and conditions who are in the cities under bombardment. Yet the Eucharist of Christian communities celebrates the liberating power of God for these very people, and that challenges in a stark and penetrating way any decision of a Christian people to declare war against another nation, more especially when that other nation is already among the less powerful and less wealthy of the world. We are called upon to ask ourselves what it is we are celebrating in the Eucharist if we are willing to exclude others from God's hospitality to the extent of considering their very lives expendable for some benefit that we see for ourselves or for those who are considered our allies because we share their interests.

It is, however, at a yet higher level of symbolism in the Eucharist that the matter becomes plainest. Jesus taught his disciples to celebrate his death and breakthrough to new life by interpreting it in the light of the Exodus memory. He directed the attention of his followers not, as he might have done, to his role as preacher, guide, healer or exorcist primarily, but to his death as the ultimate non-violent statement and the ultimate self-gift. Invited to become a Zealot leader, he chose quite explicitly and deliberately to right the wrongs of society not by killing others but by a non-violent challenge which made him vulnerable to the point of his own death. It is this that we celebrate, and it is this that we are invited to share: the conviction that there is a better way than war and force, and that this is a way of truth, community, dedication, compassion and self-gift.

Before the Constantinian establishment of the fourth century the conviction was strong and apparently universal among Christians that entry into the death and resurrection of Jesus was incompatible with any kind of participation in the killing of human beings. Subsequently compromises were made, reluctantly allowing warfare but placing restraints upon it. Some centuries later a further compromise presented the Crusades not as a reluctant compromise but as a holy and meritorious commitment—an attitude echoed in colonial expansion blessed as Christian mission, and again in wars to "contain" Communism which were understood by many as a defense of godliness, and finally in a rather broader, more vaguely defined sense of a moral and spiritual commitment to make wars to defend "our way of life" seen now as a holy thing.

In every age people come to understand and accept their faith as it is presented to them. Our sacramental encounters have become highly ritualized and formal. Participation has been possible without a deep existential grasp of the implications of our sacramental actions and symbols. It was the realization of this state of affairs that led to a reshaping of the rites in the wake of the Second Vatican Council. The immediate goal was that the signs should really signify the further goal that the community of the faithful should be revitalized in the recognition of what it is that the signs signify. The hope was and is that in this way the Eucharist might truly become what it was intended to be: a peak or summit in the lives of believers, to which everything leads and from which everything flows, a high vantage point from which everything could be seen more clearly and in its true relationships.

That task as proposed in the liturgical renewal is by no means complete in our times. The relationship of what we do in the Eucharist with what we do in our public and private lives must keep unfolding before us, and it will do this only if constant and well-informed reflection is given to it by many Christians, singly and in communities. Such reflection certainly concerns the ordering of our individual lives, our one to one relationships, our families and our work. But it does not end there. It must also take in what we do collectively in shaping our societies, how we make our democracies work, and what we do as a nation. The Eucharist signifies in its multiple symbolism that the way of Christ is peace, and that peace is possible not only in our hearts but in our world with all its ambiguities and all its complexity. Christ has given us a new share in God's hospitality in the Eucharist which is blessing, sacrament and transformation.

Questions for Discussion

1. What in your opinion is the connection between the Eucharist and peace?

2. If there is a connection, what can ordinary Christians do about it?

3. What has been most helpful about this book, and what has been most problematic?

Suggestions for Further Reading

Introduction. Two books which provide more content for the question: Does it have meaning in our lives, are: Tissa Balasuriya, *The Eucharist and Human Liberation* (Orbis, 1978), and George S. Worgul, *From Magic to Metaphor* (Paulist, 1980).

Chapter 1. A very helpful book on hunger in connection with this chapter is: Suzanne C. Toton, *World Hunger* (Orbis 1982). Another helpful "stand-by" which has become a classic is: Arthur Simon, *Bread for the World* (Paulist, 1975).

Chapter 2. The hunger for freedom and dignity is well set out in Phillip Berryman, *Liberation Theology* (Pantheon, 1987), and is discussed authoritatively and seriously in two encyclical letters of Pope John Paul II: *Redemptor hominis (Redeemer of Man)* and *Laborem exercens (On Human Work).*

Chapter 3. Very moving testimonies on this theme from the church of the earliest centuries, during times of persecution are available in: Willy Rordorf, et al., *The Eucharist of the Early Christians* (Liturgical Press, Pueblo, 1976).

Chapter 4. Two books that offer extensive follow-up to the issues raised in this chapter are: Leo Hay, *Eucharist, a Thanksgiving Celebration* (Liturgical Press, Glazier, 1989), and *Eucharist and Eschatology,* Geoffrey Wainwright (Oxford University Press, 1981).

Chapter 5. A book which amplifies this material and is easy to read and understand is: Regis Duffy, *Real Presence* (Harper & Row, 1982). For those with more technical questions related to pre-Vatican II understandings, a very helpful book is: Edward Schillebeeckx, *The Eucharist* (Sheed & Ward, 1968).

Chapter 6. Particularly helpful in connection with the link of this chapter with the tradition is: Nicholas Lash, *His Presence in the World* (Pflaum, 1968), available in libraries only.

Chapter 7. Especially helpful in showing the foundation for the Christian mission to the hungry of the world is: Ronald J. Sider, *Cry Justice: The Bible on Hunger and Poverty* (Paulist, 1980). A further explanation is available in Julio de Santa Ana, *Good News to the Poor* (Orbis, 1979).

Chapter 8. Much has been written on peace as a Christian imperative. Attention should perhaps be drawn once again to two papal encyclical letters: *Pacem in Terris (Peace on Earth)* of Pope John XXIII, and *Populorum Progressio (On the Development of Peoples)* of Pope Paul VI.